PRAISE FOR
UNDER MY ROOF

"*Under My Roof* is a courageous, at times compelling, honest and informative narrative. King's well-crafted, all-too-familiar images present a fresh insight despite the major challenges of the thinking in this field and in the law."

–*Diane Bridgeman*, Ph.D., Licensed Psychologist, Chair of the American Psychological Association's Advisory Committee on Colleague Assistance, and Chair of the California Disaster Mental Health Coalition

"*Under My Roof* is a brave, compelling and necessary story of one mother's attempt to protect her daughter in an era before there was real help available. We have very few accounts of incest from the perspective of the mother, and Emalou King has given us a heartbreakingly honest book that takes us through the suffering and into healing. This story will be supportive for all mothers whose children have been abused; for all survivors of abuse who want to understand more about their mothers, and it should be required reading for every professional who works with families in which incest has taken place."

–*Ellen Bass*, Author of *The Courage to Heal: A Guide for Women Survivors of Child Sexual Abuse* (HarperCollins 1983)co-authored with Laura Davis; and, *The Human Line* (Copper Canyon Press, 2007); *Mules of Love* (BOA, 2002) which won the Lambda Literary Award; Featured on the March/April 2011 cover of the *American Poetry Review*.

"*Under My Roof* is an outstanding contribution, and King being a nurse adds to the cache. This is a fresh point of view . . ."

–*Marla Miller*, April 18, 2011, *The Writer Magazine*; Founder, MarketingTheMuse.com

UNDER MY ROOF

UNDER MY ROOF

A *Mother's* Story of the Heinous Crime of Incest

Emalou King, RN, BSN, Phn

SIX DEGREES PUBLISHING GROUP
PORTLAND • OREGON
USA

UNDER MY ROOF
A *Mother's* Story of the Heinous Crime of Incest
Second Edition

Emalou King, RN, BSN, Phn

PUBLISHED BY SIX DEGREES PUBLISHING GROUP
5320 Macadam, Suite 100
Portland, OR 97239 USA

ISBN: 978-0-9856048-3-7
ISBN 978-4524-8148-7 (digital)

Library of Congress Location Number: 2013948349

Front Cover: Judy Bullard
A first edition of this book was published in 2011.
Inquiries and Permissions: email Publisher@SixDegreesPublishing.com
www.SixDegreesPublishing.com

Author's note: This work is a Memoir. This story authentically reflects the author's present recollection of her experiences of a 20-year period in her life. Certain names, locations and identifying characteristics have been changed, and certain individuals are composites. Dialogue and events have been recreated from memory, and in some cases, have been compressed to convey the substance of what was said or what occurred.

Publisher's note: Included in this Second Edition of *Under My Roof* is both a resource guide and a series of reflective questions developed by the author meant to assist the reader, study group and/or book club facilitator by opening the conversation about the recognition of the signs of sexual abuse, bringing an end to it and beginning the healing process. Neither are meant to take the place of professional counseling.

Printed simultaneously in the United States of America, Australia, and the UK
1 3 5 7 9 10 8 6 4 2

This book is dedicated to survivors and their mothers
with hope for healing of their wounded souls.

~ ❦ ~

Contents

Foreword   xi

Acknowledgments   xiii

Introduction   xv

Saturday, March 7, 1964   1
  Summer at Home
  Back to School
June 3, 1965   13
  August 21, 1965
  Our Place and Pregnancy
  My First Job
Our New Addition   26
  Viet Nam/Thailand Tour
Our New Home in Germany   32
  The NCO Wives Club Welcoming
  Strike One
The Accident   38
  The Investigation
  Jackpot
  Hippies
My Heartaches   48
  All of Our Problems and More
  Base Housing
  My English Friend
  Soon . . . It Will Be Soon
The Military Inspections   60
  Stop the Crying
  The Move
Going Stateside   64
  House Hunting
  The Next Move
  Ray's Shop
Wired Shut   73
  The Call for Help
  Jimmy's Accident

Life On Ewing Street
What Eats Away at Me   81
    The Birds and the Bees
    Fixing Up the Place
    Monday Was Wash Day
    Acting Out
Under My Roof   90
    Today's Mail
    The Call
    Therapy
    After Therapy
    Changes
Prom   103
    Mother's Short Visit
    Rained Out
    The Nurses Convention
The Promise   110
    Off to School
    The Unexpected
    November 1984 – My Cry for Help
The Plan   121
    The Intervention
    Merry Christmas
    Happy New Year 1985
The Call   131
    What Else Is Going On . . .?
    The Art of Persuasion
    Family Week
    Orientation
    Treatment
    Cleaning House
The Divorce   146
The Sentencing   147
    The Altercation
    The Answer to My Prayers
    One Day at a Time
Try to Erase the Past   151

Epilogue   155
Afterword   159
Resources   160
Readers' Conversation Guide   161
About the Author   169

Foreword

In more than one way, *Under My Roof* reminds me of a mystery novel. The memoir begins like innumerable accounts of dating, romance and eventual marriage in America. The only hint of trouble to come is dislike of Emma's parents for Ray, their soon-to-be son-in-law, a not unheard of response. As the story unfolds, there are more intimations of trouble to come—drunkenness, a terrible accident—but nothing to prepare us for the scene revealing a heartbreaking and most heinous evil.

We see this family develop through the eyes of the mother. We feel with her an unease with the moods, anger and drinking of her spouse. Routine and apparent normalcy keep the family going, just as it does in our own lives. Ray has some likable but strange parents—another tiny hint of the horror to come?—and his faults, but nothing indicative of molestation. Would to God molesters appear as the criminals they are! Alas, they look like regular guys. Like the clever murderer at the center of a mystery, Ray manages to disguise his methods of manipulation in pursuit of his perversion.

If we can believe the astounding number of children now being molested—most of them victimized by members of their own families—this book is both necessary and, to use a strange word, comforting. *Under My Roof* is necessary because it teaches us how insidious and damaging molestation is and how relentless and devious the familial perpetrator can be. The memoir is comforting because Emma is so much like ourselves: raising her kids, struggling with her husband's apparent weaknesses but understandably missing what he took such pains to hide.

Under My Roof is also comforting in that abuse and its attendant agony and pain do not have to have the last word:

Faith in God contributes to the healing, which begins slowly and wonderfully to unfold.

Parents, teenagers, teachers, clergy, counselors and people in law enforcement would surely benefit from reading this book. Conversational in style, *Under My Roof* gets under the skin as well as startling and moving the heart. I found Emma's story gripping and the book difficult to put down. I hope and pray *Under My Roof* has a wide readership.

Fr. Patrick J. Dooling
Diocese of Monterey

Acknowledgments

God comes first, and then I am grateful to my family, close friends and colleagues, plus my Al-Anon sponsor and my parish priest, who supported me in telling MY story.

A special thanks to fellow students in the Thursday afternoon Ellen Bass class for writers. The advice and feedback was most helpful.

I need to acknowledge the support from the agents, editors and other authors at the San Francisco Writers' Conference.

Thank you to 12-Step Drug Treatment facilities across the country and their intervention techniques, as well as the Survivor's Healing Center for the victims of sexual abuse whose staff continue to raise awareness in the communities through education, recognition and the media.

I am especially thankful to Six Degrees Publishing Group, who also saw the need to open eyes and give a voice to mothers of survivors of these sex crimes.

–Emalou King

Introduction

As a society, we have under-reacted and under-estimated the scope of the problem of childhood sexual abuse. When the first edition of *Under My Roof* was released as an ebook in 2011, my purpose was to portray how this heinous crime happens in a home—from a *mother's* perspective. The book provided a venue for expression of the secret, unspoken and buried parts of people's lives. The story was meant to open eyes and ears by providing an environment and opportunity for sharing and healing.

One day while at the grocery store, a retired sheriff who had read *Under My Roof* stopped me and said, "After reading your book, a woman found the courage to report a crime of sexual abuse." I was ecstatic to hear that—so much so that I forgot what I had gone into the store to buy.

On another day while out shopping with two women friends, I told them the name of my memoir. Each looked surprised by the title and immediately revealed their experiences of being molested—one by a neighbor and the other by an uncle. Neither had shared their experience with their mothers. Since this book was originally released, I have heard about domestic abuse involving fathers, uncles, adoptions and first marriages, including several rapes, incestuous siblings and sadly, abortions.

During the same time period this ebook was being released, Penn State held a dark secret of its own: The crimes of the assistant coach and serial child molester, Jerry Sandusky. It wasn't until 2012 that thirty years of child abuse perpetrated by Jerry Sandusky came to light and was headlined in the news night after night. His outrageous and abusive behavior triggered everyone who had ever been molested. It opened the wounds of all those who had disclosed or kept secret what had happened to them. I was angry. The country was angry. At that time, I contacted my publisher and we knew it was time to reach out to more people—those who didn't have or use a computer or preferred a paper edition.

Today it is impossible to check social media sites, iPhones, iPads, Facebook, TV, radio or newspapers and not read something about sexual abuse. The award-winning film, *The Invisible War,* a documentary about sexual abuse in the United States military, claimed that rape was considered an occupational hazard. In June of 2013, The Senate Armed Services Committee met to discuss sexual misconduct within the military in light of the recent Department of Defense statistics released which estimated 26,000 assaults in 2012 of both women and men, an increase of 35% from 2010. It was estimated that 90% of the sexual assaults are never reported because of fear of retaliation. Reasons given include that the person in charge was a "friend" of the rapist or the person in charge was the rapist. There are no convicted felony sex offenders in the military because sex offenders plead down like a "catch and release" program. Once released from the military and returned to civilian life, they become even more capable of perpetrating sexual crimes and more dangerous.

Slavery has ended? Issues of control and violence still exist in our culture. In June 2013, PBSs *Frontline* aired a segment about the sexual exploitation of migrant field workers in the United States called *Rape in the Fields*. The news story was released by PBS in both English and Spanish. Crops in the story were referred to as the "field of panties." At the time of the airing of this news documentary, no criminal prosecutions had been brought forward by farm workers and no reliable statistics were available. It is clearly a huge problem and hardship for the victims.

It is wrong to accept the unacceptable! I need to repeat that. ***It is wrong to accept the unacceptable.*** Really, it is much the same way as it works with alcoholism and dysfunctional relationships: The first time something is upsetting . . . next time the same . . . and the same . . . then it's the norm.

The sex offender leads a double life. Molesters are picky—

they don't molest everybody. They carefully choose and set up their victims. Any place there is a speck of privacy presents an opportunity. The well-planned process of *grooming* is done over a long period of time.

Did you know? A judge can remove a child from an unoffending mother and give him to the sexually abusing father. These are not isolated cases. Did you know? Not all court hearings have court reporters. Did you know? A court reporter may cost $300 per standard session and more for extended sessions. Did you know? In some counties, when a child has a court-ordered supervised visit, the parent who is getting to see the child must pay $100 for each visit? Three visits a week can be a financial hardship.

Have a 'no secrets rule' in your house. Take your child for a checkup if a child complains of symptoms and make sure you tell the doctor what you suspect so that it is documented. Let your child know they did nothing wrong and tell them how courageous they have been to tell you what happened. The doctor, nurses, police and teachers are mandated reporters. Get help.

Since the release of the first edition of *Under My Roof*, I have become a "Friend of the Survivors Healing Center" of Santa Cruz, California, participated in the "Walk to Stop the Silence" parade, set up a table in several parks, helped with fundraising and spoken to a work group. I have also participated as a panelist in a recovery program.

By purchasing a copy of this book, you are supporting programs that promote healing for the unoffending parent, siblings and the survivor. Royalties from the sales of *Under My Roof* have been and will continue to be given to the Survivor's Healing Center of Santa Cruz, California. Now, *Under My Roof*, Second Edition is in full distribution in bookstores and available to libraries and is still available in ebook format. Hopefully you begin the conversation or gift this book. Please continue to help "Stop the Silence."

Thank you first, always to God . . .
Emalou King, RN, BSN, Phn

The ultimate therapy is to identify our own pain with the pain of others, and then band together to resist the conditions that create our common malady.
–Parker Palmer

My parents told me not to marry Ray. Last night, I drifted off with clips of that nightmare running on the inside of my eyelids like a movie strip. The film snapped, clicked like hiccups and woke me. I remembered the smell of his breath, the tone of his voice and his piercing stare. Out of habit, I scanned the obits for his name and finished my coffee.

Saturday, March 7, 1964

I was a twenty-year-old senior nursing student, attending a Midwestern Catholic school with a dorm curfew of 11:00 p.m. on the weekends. After I finished my mid-term paper on cystic fibrosis, I celebrated by doubling on my first blind date with Zoe, my roommate, who dated Frank. Frank lived across the street from a boy named Ray, and they thought Ray would be perfect for me. And because I believed in my mother's romantic gene that you were *". . . nobody till somebody loved you,"* I was game.

"Emma, are you ready?"

"Almost, but do I look okay in this dress, Zoe?"

"Yes. For the tenth time, you look fine and Ray will like you."

Frank arrived alone in a turquoise car that matched both his eyes and his shirt.

"Where's my date?" I asked.

"We have to pick him up. He's at work. I thought you knew," Frank said.

He pulled up the curved driveway, revved the engine, and then it purred. I was nervous and giggled when Frank did it again, drawing the attention of the couple coming through the rotating doors. Ray was finishing his shift at the hotel where he bellhopped. Five minutes later, I watched this tall, clean-cut guy swagger out to the car like he owned the hotel. He greeted Frank and Zoe and chatted with them until I boldly cleared my throat and extended my hand.

"Oh, pardon me," said Frank. "Ray, this is Emma; Emma . . . *Ray*."

Ray's denim-blue eyes studied my face before he kissed the tops of my fingers. That's all he did and something happened. When Ray slid next to me in the back seat, the air was warm and electrifying and his intoxicating scent swallowed me alive. Frank winked at me in the rear view mirror, and I regained my composure, thankful I didn't giggle. My aunt once said, "When love hits you like that, it's a true thing." I never argued with her.

The first hour of our Saturday afternoon date was in a basement on the East side of town, where Frank supervised slot car races with a group of young Boy Scouts. I wasn't exactly the quiet type, but today was different. I watched as Ray saluted Frank, moved away from the excited bunch of boys, and leaned against a workbench. He didn't seem interested in the toy action; instead, he beckoned Zoe over, looked her up and down, laughed with her and shifted from one foot to the other. She had flaming red hair and breasts that filled her sweater. I noticed my own reflection in the mirror, smoothed the front of my red shirtdress and fingered my pearls like rosary beads. I stood by Frank and cheered for the boys who won.

When the races were over, we recoupled and went for cheeseburgers and malts, dragged the strip, parked and talked. In the back seat, Ray patted the top of his leg and gave a nod for me to slide over next to him. I did it naturally, like I belonged there. I fit nicely under the protection of his arm. At the end of the date, he smiled and kissed me good night like I had never been kissed. Our bodies melded together briefly, and the sparks flew right through our clothing.

"Hey Zoe," I asked after lights out. "What's Ray's last name?"

"I don't know," she whispered. "Didn't you ask him?"

"No, but I know for sure that Ray's the one. I'm going to marry him someday. I should at least find out his name!"

"Omigod; you're in love!" Zoe sighed and pulled the covers up over her head. "Go to sleep."

Sleeping was difficult because I relived each moment of our date thinking about Ray. In the morning I was glassy-eyed and skipped breakfast. Later I snacked at the hospital cafeteria on vanilla ice cream smeared on saltine crackers. When my instructor asked why I flunked my test, I grinned.

Our dorm room on the second floor looked out onto the street. I sat on the edge of my bed and counted every car that passed. I thought I saw Ray drive by, but it was two weeks before he phoned. I quivered when I heard his voice. No one affected me like he did—like a drug. His words soaked into my ears like music. It was wonderfully frightening, this falling in love, and I smiled like an idiot at the mention of his name.

Next date, we rushed off to a movie in the middle of the afternoon. We walked in during the previews and sat near the back. It was too dark to see anyone else. We held hands, and once in awhile, Ray's lips brushed my cheek when he whispered something.

When the movie ended, we were in the midst of an entire theatre of crutches, walkers and wheelchairs. The large posters advertised a special matinée benefit for the handicapped. Now I understood the funny look from the usher. Ray grabbed my shoulder and began to drag his leg behind him, faking paralysis. I became his supporting actor while Ray did this drag, step, drag, step routine.

"Are we out of sight yet?" he said.

"Yes. They can't see us now. What got into you?"

"Well, I didn't want them to feel bad, being crippled and stuff. Hey, this calls for a drink. I'll show you a secret place."

"Ray, I'm not old enough."

"Oh, don't worry; I know everyone," he said.

We slipped into a narrow little bar stuck between two tall buildings, a place lawyers and judges would adjourn to after hours. Ray had little tufts of premature gray hair behind his ears that he called *Mormon horns*. I had no idea his age because he seemed worldly. Ray filled in bartending when they were short of help. He had lived by the ocean and spoke Russian. I had never seen the ocean, couldn't even speak Pig Latin and had only been to Idaho. We sat in the darkened corner holding hands, and I got woozy on one gin and tonic. Ray drank a couple of scotch and sodas and played a song with that same name on the jukebox.

On our next date, Ray invited me home for dinner. I wore my best yellow and green plaid box-pleated skirt with a matching jacket. Ray looked nice in gray slacks and a blue shirt. He parked the '57 Chevy behind his dad's woody wagon in the driveway in front of their garage. They lived in a tract house in a new development of town with scrubby grass under a two-foot pine tree. His dad worked construction and his mother managed the books in a real estate office.

Up the street several kids played catch. Out from that yard came A-bomb, a bloodhound dog that hung so low to the ground his stuff touched the sidewalk. A-bomb dragged his jewels slowly across the cement right over to my feet. I'm sure my face turned red and I stepped back. Ray muttered, "That damn dog . . . don't even pet him."

Ray wrapped his arm around my waist and we walked up the steps. He tried to peek through the steamed-over window, and immediately, his mother opened the front door and smiled.

Sophie was a short busty woman with bare arms and a tiny bit of her bra strap showing under her yellow cobbler apron—the kind my grandmother wore. Her wire rims rested on a small nose, and dyed-brown, spidery hair partially covered her high forehead. Sophie reached up, hugged her son first and welcomed me. George appeared from a hallway off the dining room. He was small-framed with a muscular stature, reminding me more of a cowboy, and nothing like his son. He had pressed clothes, a western belt buckle, shined boots and the fragrance of Old Spice.

"Well, hello there," he said. "I'm the runt, but I have a big twin brother."

When I laughed, Ray nudged me and said, "No really; he has a big twin." I laughed again. My mother was an identical twin.

Before dinner, his parents each drank a tumbler of whiskey. Ray and I had sodas. George fiddled around in a drawer below the wall telephone and took out two pill bottles. He tipped each bottle into his hand, threw a few striped capsules in his mouth, swallowed his whiskey and mumbled something about back pain. Shortly thereafter, he sang.

Watching George was like watching a whirlwind. He put the vacuum cleaner away, shoved the piano bench in and pointed to the Chinese hangings against the white wall. "I did the beadwork," he said and turned off the television.

The galley kitchen was cute with teapot wallpaper and café curtains. Bowls of ripened fruit and a bottle of Milk of Magnesia sat on the counter by a half-opened package of Fig Newton cookies. Paper sacks poked out above the refrigerator. In only four giant steps, we were in the garage messing with fishing tackle and worms. George showed off his antique radio and hummed between our conversations.

Pork roast and potato aromas filled the whole house. Sophie opened canned applesauce and forked out watermelon pickles. Ray sliced and mashed, and I put the white bread and the covered butter dish in the center of the oilcloth.

We made the sign of the cross, bowed our heads and said

grace. Ray looked at me tenderly and touched my leg under the table. My face felt prickly around my ears and I pushed his hand away. George talked through the whole meal. In one of those rare quiet moments, Sophie told us she hated contour sheets because she was too short to fold one all by herself. Then it was back to George again and gardening. Sophie forgot to serve the string beans and remembered after the chocolate ice cream sundaes.

"You're like the daughter we don't have," Sophie said leaning on her elbows.

"Yeah," Ray said. "They didn't want me. Told me I was the ugliest baby they had ever seen."

"You . . . *ugly*? That's hard to believe."

"Yes he was," said his dad. "He looked like an old man . . . all red and wrinkled . . . plain ugly."

"It's a family joke," Sophie said and stood up behind Ray. She put her arms around his neck, kissed his cheek and whispered. When they both laughed, I thought it was rude and I was uncomfortable. They had secrets . . .

George whistled, ignored them, ambled back into the kitchen and took another nip of whiskey. That's when Ginger rescued me. She dropped her toy at my feet. It was a tennis ball inside a tube sock. I reached down and Ginger grabbed the other end between her teeth and pulled. When she growled with pleasure, Ray got the sock away and they tugged. They laughed and played.

My aunt told me if a man loves his mother and his dog, he's a good man. I thought she was spot on.

Summer at Home

During the summer months back home, I worked at Mercy Hospital as a student nurse and discovered the nurses' aides and the janitors were most helpful to know. I gave bed baths, delivered trays, and sometimes helped with minor procedures. It was exciting. I loved the hospital environment—the marble floors and white walls, the zing of the curtains on the rails, the rubber call bells, the hopper sounds, the rubbing alcohol scent and hospital cafeteria food. There was sacredness about this space that spread beyond the hospital chapel. Everyone respected and appreciated the nurses and I had wanted to be a nurse ever since I was a child.

~~~~

One day after work, I got a surprise phone call from Ray. He had driven 363 miles to see me and called from a motel on the west side of town. He came to take me out for a lunch date, but when I asked my parents, they insisted Ray come to the house and have a chilled shrimp salad and fresh blueberry muffin lunch with us out on our enclosed patio. They wanted to meet the boy who astounded me.

My parents were very polite when introduced, and even though Ray had a good solid handshake, my father backed up eyeing him from head to toe like a fire inspector. Ray was so nervous around them that, within the hour, he choked on a piece of shrimp, and my parents stood up to pat him on the back and get him some water. He was very embarrassed, and I felt bad for him. It was hard to tell if they liked him. Ray was quite the talker on any subject.

After we dragged Main Street a few times, there wasn't much else to do, so when we heard on the radio that there was a flood in Canada and people were to stay put and be careful, we decided to check it out for ourselves. We crossed the border without our parents' permission and came back without them knowing where we had spent several hours. We had been kissing a lot before I came in at three o'clock in the morning, so I straightened my matted hair and clothes before I walked in the door, hoping Mom and Dad were asleep.

Ray left the next day and promised to call and write and see me in the fall for my senior year. I was ecstatic, but my parents were quiet—something about him they didn't like. Neither one of them could put a finger on it, but they didn't trust him and certainly didn't want their daughter to date him. They hoped it would all blow over.

Then an occurrence made the situation even worse—one that validated my parent's sense of who this person was underneath the bullshit facade of words.

Each day, I waited for the mail. Today when I tore open my letter from Ray, the salutation was *"Dear Penney."* I turned the envelope back over, thinking I had opened someone else's mail, and nearly panicked because I knew that was a federal offense. I quickly put the paper back into the envelope, took the letter into my room, and sat on my bed. *Okay,* I thought, *my name is on the envelope so it is my letter. Whatever is written on the paper is something for me to know.* I took the folded single sheet of paper in Ray's handwriting out of the envelope and read words that didn't make any sense. The lump in my throat got bigger and my mouth was watery, like right before you puke. It said words like, *"I am sorry "... "Pregnant" ... "plans for the baby."*

I slid off my bed onto the floor and pulled my bedspread up over my head, and then I twisted myself into a long tube and screamed. I kicked the floor with my heels so hard the thud sounds brought my mother instantly pounding on my bedroom door.

"Emma, what's the matter?"

I screamed louder.

"Unlock your door right now."

"No. I can't. I don't want to talk to anybody."

"What happened, honey?"

"Go away, Mom."

"No. Open the door—right now. Do you hear me?"

I held the letter behind my back. My face was wet, my eyes swollen and my nose plugged. My mother put her arms around me and patted my back.

"Let me see what's wrong ..."

"Ray sent me a letter that doesn't belong to me. I don't know why I have it. He sent a letter to me that belongs to a girl named

Penney. I read it, Mom. I wish I hadn't, but I read it. Now what do I do?"

"About what, Emma?" Mom unfolded the letter, her eyebrows raised, her lips tightened. She shook her head back and forth.

"Ray . . . I need to talk to Ray right now."

"No, Emma. You're too upset. And besides, you hardly know this man or what he'll do."

"Mom, I love him," and I started crying again.

"Give me his phone number," Mom said then carefully descended into the basement for privacy and made the call to his parents. They talked for a long time, and when Mom came back upstairs, she looked tired.

"It's all true. Ray got Penney pregnant. And, young lady, you might want to rethink your plans."

"No. We can make things work." When I slammed my door, it marked hardened hearts for my mother and me for the next few months. It was true that Ray got a girl pregnant down South when he was away at school way before I met him, but the teen mother gave the baby girl up for adoption. That topic of conversation lasted one day at our house. Since I still wouldn't back off, the subject dropped off the radar. When I look back on this, I didn't "Honor Thy Mother and Thy Father" like the Commandment said.

Back to School

I traveled back to school in September. Mother rode in the back seat of the car and cried the entire way, while I sat up in front with my dad. When I arrived at school, my dad took my bags to my room; I gave him a peck on the cheek and a hug, and they left. I couldn't wait to see Ray. He came to my dorm right after dinner but we didn't go out. He brought his friend along who hung around at the bottom of the tall stairs in the front of the dorm. Ray kissed me and then told me that he wasn't good enough for me and we shouldn't date. After that kiss, no way I was letting him go. We made plans for a weekend movie.

~~~~

Sophie scheduled Ray for an angiogram because of his frequent headaches that sometimes hurt so bad that he hit things. During these episodes he had to be alone and in the dark and bite on something, so his doctor wanted to rule out a brain tumor.

The day arrived for Ray's surgical procedure. I looked in on him afterwards. As I stepped off the elevator in my student uniform, I peered in from the doorway. A blonde woman sitting across from his bed stood when she saw me. Ray, groggy, slowly opened his eyes. She took his hand, leaned over him and said good-bye. "Nice to meet you," she mumbled to me when she left, but no one had introduced us.

"Hi, Ray. How ya doing?" I asked.

"They say I can't move my head. Come closer," he slurred.

I moved next to his bed where the lingering scent of ether caught my breath. He drifted in and out of sleep from the anesthetic, looking peaceful, and gentle with reddish eyelashes. During this quiet time, he opened his eyes, simply asked me to marry him, and closed them again. *He proposed.* I didn't know if he meant it or if it was the effect of the drugs. I was still smiling when Sister Mary Frances stood in the doorway, tapped her finger on the little watch that she magically pulled from her tunic, and kicked me out. My cheeks flushed.

"Take care, Ray. Good night."

Before our marriage, when I could have cut it off like my parents wanted me to do, I didn't.

Ray and I slipped into his bedroom so he could get something before we went out on our date. He had his back turned and asked me to get his cufflinks out of his jewelry box. That's when I saw something I thought I wasn't supposed to see, or maybe that was the plan all along. I found his cufflinks under a faded Polaroid photo of a naked girl posed on a bed. Behind her was one of those silly tall bottles covered with a knitted pink poodle.

She was probably only a sophomore in high school, and I knew who she was looking at—who was behind the camera—because I looked at him that same way; and I immediately disliked her and her poodle bottle.

Ray cleared his throat—I handed him the cufflinks and turned the picture back upside down.

"That's Penney, my old girlfriend back East, but we don't have contact any more. I forgot I still had that picture."

"Oh. Did you take the picture, Ray?"

"Yeah."

"*Oooohhh*." And then I knew I was supposed to find it and see that Penney had little boobies and sun-bleached blonde hair.

We walked into Maroons, a local hangout, on our fourth date. Ray, unusually quiet, chugged his coke. He tapped his fingers on the table to the music from the Jukebox and tickled my palm. Mom told me that a boy who does that is *nasty*. I didn't know what it meant, so pulled my hand away, rubbed it on my skirt and figured it wouldn't count. That was my interpretation of the five-second rule.

"Thanks for visiting me last night," Ray said.

"Did you get your results yet?" I asked between songs.

"Yeah, but let's get out of here," he said, pulling on my sweater sleeve.

"Ray, I only have an hour. I have to be in the dorm."

"I know," he said. "I'll get you back."

"Well, what did the doctor say?"

Ray parked the car overlooking the city, took out a furry box and handed it to me. Unsuspecting, I flipped it open like a hard pack of cigarettes.

"*Oooomigod*!"

"Will you marry me?" he asked.

In my excitement, I spilled my cola in his lap. Ray jumped, cussed and was angry.

"I'm sorry, I'm sorry."

He wiped himself off with a small rag from the gin box and tossed it out the window. The strong wind swept it up and over the edge of the rims. "Let's try this again," he said, disappointed.

"Okay." I closed the box and opened it slowly. It was an exquisite white gold one-carat diamond ring.

"Now, Emma, will you marry me?"

"Yes, yes, yes . . ."

Ray kissed me and every cell in my body opened up in pure joy. We kissed until I felt drugged.

"You better get me back before I'm in trouble," I whispered between his kisses.

"Oh honey, I've got something else to tell you."

"Anything," I said breathless, straightening my hair.

"I don't have a brain tumor. That's the good news. But I've joined the Air Force with my friend, Bob. We're going in under the new buddy system."

"What? . . . You're *leaving*?"

"Not for a couple of months. I've thought this through. It's a good deal, Emma. After Basic we can get married and you know . . ." he paused, running the tip of his tongue across my lips. I pulled back, twisted my new ring on my finger, held my hand up to the light and admired the sparkle.

"And then we can live happily ever after?" I giggled.

"Sure . . . trust me."

"Ray, I was meaning to ask you, who was that woman who left when I came into your room at the hospital?"

"Oh it's just an old friend . . . not a girlfriend. I babysit her daughter when she can't find anyone. We went to the movies a few times and stuff like that, that's all."

"So you like kids?"

"Sure I do." He squeezed my hand and started the car.

We spent every possible minute together. My heart ached when I thought about Ray leaving. He reminded me time apart would go fast and that I had a ton of schoolwork before graduation.

We never stopped talking when we were together, except for the kissing that happened, usually right before he took me back to the dorm. We covered the alphabet from circumcision to clothes styles. Ray said he abhorred sweatshirts on girls. He didn't wear them or jeans, because blue jeans made ingrown hairs on his legs. I loved my comfortable warm sweatshirts and collected them from different schools. Then he requested I never wear them again. So I agreed not to, but I didn't want to say that. What was it . . . the look on his face, his voice or his touch that persuaded me? I made Ray a promise, even though he would be away at Basic Training. And I kept my word. My little sister got all of them. I thought I was being nice and my mother, surprised by this grand gesture, agreed. But I wasn't—I was already obedient. So I only got rid of *them,* so I could have *him.* This was a test I didn't want to fail. He cared about what I wore. No one else did—except my parents, who loved me.

I waved and blew kisses until the bus for Biloxi, Mississippi was out of sight. I held back tears, and Sophie treated me to lunch before I returned to my dorm. Ray's letters arrived daily with pictures. I read and re-read them, kissed the picture of his shaved head and yearned for his return. I liked what Connie Francis sang, " . . . *if it takes forever, I will wait for you, for a thousand summers . . .*"

I visited his parents' house and studied in Ray's bedroom. I opened his closet to touch his clothes and feel closer to him. His scent lingered on his red and white pinstriped shirt. I buried my nose deep in the material and sucked up memories.

June 3, 1965

It was the last social get-together for the fifteen of us in my class. Our nursing instructors gave us a graduation party at one of their homes. The teachers provided a banquet of their favorite dishes. After the celebration, several of us piled into the first car, and my friend, Joanie, sat on my lap in the back seat behind the driver.

The pelting rain made the streets slick and it was getting dark. We were four houses down the street, halfway through the intersection, when a car broadsided us. Metal ground on metal. We spun out of control. The impact whipped my head back against the seat, and my empty arms fell to my sides. Joanie disappeared through the sprung door. For a second, *eerie silence* . . . and then moans. The stink of burning rubber shocked my nostrils. I crawled out from the back seat and yelled for Joanie, but she didn't answer. Her body had slammed into a parked, red jeep and dropped to the ground. She lay in the street on her side, the same way she slept in her bed. The classmates in the car behind us witnessed the horror. Our teachers ran out from their house when they heard the crash. A few knelt over Joanie while the others tended to the injured from my car until the ambulance arrived.

The sirens hurt my ears. I mumbled, *"Shit, shit, shit, shit."* No one noticed me. Too many people gathered around and I didn't know what to do. Where was my cigarette lighter from Ray? It was missing. I patted around on the ground under the shadow of the streetlight, looked under the car and on the back seat and floor. I sat on the curb and picked chunks of glass out of my hair. Then an officer asked if I needed help. That's right when I spotted the shiny square in a patch of lawn and lit my cigarette.

The first ambulance whisked Joanie away, and I thought that meant she'd be okay. I ran my thumb over the engraving on my lighter like a silent mantra, back and forth, back and forth . . . each groove a prayer. I always prayed when something went wrong, before I took a test, and before I ate my meals. Then out of my mouth came the first prayer I ever learned from my mother when I was four, *"Jesus, Mary and Joseph, I place all my trust in You."*

Since I looked uninjured and was in the way, I stood next to the police car with Sarah, the driver of our mangled automobile. When I wanted to talk, she put her finger up to her lips to shush me and took my hand.

"Have you been drinking?" The officer asked looking over his shoulder.

We slid closer together, shook our heads no, and cried dry with our mouths closed.

"How old are you girls anyway?" We still didn't answer. "Okay, we'll get you to talk downtown."

The police used code words on their radio, and when we arrived, separated us into little rooms for interrogation, like criminals. I wanted my dad. I called my parents from the police station. They were glad I was okay. But I didn't mean okay . . . I was awful. I needed them—at least to stay on the phone and talk to me. But they hung up. They didn't make anything better, except they arranged a ride from the police station back to the darkened dorm connected to the hospital.

I burst through the doors of the Emergency Room out of breath and into the bright lights.

One teacher approached me from the front, the other from the side. "*Joanie is dead,*" they said in unison.

When I opened my mouth wide to scream, Mrs. Hart stuffed it with a washcloth and muffled my sounds. "*Shhh!*" she whispered, holding me and rocking me. I started to fold and was lowered to a chair with her hands resting on my shoulders. When I stopped making sounds, she told me to remove the washcloth and sit quietly with the rest of my class. We huddled together and quivered without words . . . *so that's what dead silence means*!

I stood in the center of the exam room amidst equipment, tubes, wires and blood after Joanie's body was released to the morgue. By the looks of the room, they must have tried everything; but none of this seemed real, because only yesterday I assisted while the doctor pulled off a bottle of fluids from a young woman's collapsed lung in the ER and saved her. Didn't they try that? I closed the door, sat in the corner on the floor and let my involuntary sobs come in spasms . . . *Oh please, God; I'd like to wake up now.*

The accident hit the morning paper's front page. The driver's name was wrong; it didn't happen like they said it did, and I should know—I was there, and I was angry.

Ray wouldn't make it home for the funeral or my graduation because he saved his leave for our August wedding. George and Sophie didn't comfort me like I hoped they would. Instead, they snapped pictures of the wrecked car to send to Ray. I leaned against the chain link fence and watched them—this was sick. I didn't understand adults' thinking most of the time.

Joanie was the only one in our class of graduates who had all her belongings packed to go home, so when her family came to the dorm, they took her suitcase and a box and left within minutes. Most of us hadn't even started to pack and certainly weren't ready to leave immediately. I finally closed my suitcase and wondered when and how I would die and if anyone would ever remember me. I wrote my initials on the inside of my closet so someone would know I once belonged. I swore I'd pray at Mass for Joanie's soul for the rest of my life.

The day after a solemn graduation, we drove in a caravan 144 miles to Joanie's funeral. We formed an honor guard behind her casket, sat together in the front row and sang the Mass. Fourteen young women in crisp, white uniforms, starched caps and polished shoes. Our dark navy nursing capes, folded at the shoulder, exposed the red lining. It was hard to hold our composure, but somehow in those sacred moments, out of respect for the family, we managed.

During the funeral, I heard Joanie singing. I did not mention it because someone would have thought I was nuts. Then a stranger asked me after the funeral which one of us had that angelic voice. And I told her it was Joanie. She hugged me.

The *only* shade tree in the whole cemetery was over Joanie's burial plot where the sun reflected off the leaves and made a shadow on the fresh dirt—just the way she would have wanted it. Joanie sunbathed, covered in newspapers, on the rooftop of the dorm. She loved the shade; she was sweetness and funny personified.

&

After graduation, I lived with my parents and worked the night shift at the hospital. I slept most of the day, hardly helping around the house. The sounds of the thud and the impact of the car frequently jerked me awake, and I'd sit up, slow down my breathing and wipe the tears off on my pillowcase. Three *Hail Marys* later, I was back asleep.

Then I had a bad streak.

First, I accidentally poked myself with a contaminated needle, got infectious hepatitis and spent thirty-one days in isolation at Mercy. I was thin as a napkin in my paper gown, weak and yellowish, eating off cardboard plates and sleeping for long hours. My mother sat every day for several hours in a straight-back chair six feet from my bed, wearing protective covering over her clothes and face. My beloved grandmother died in this very room—Room Number 320—ten years prior, and oddly, it was comforting and went unspoken.

Second, I missed taking my state board exams because of my month-long hospitalization. Someone called me on the phone and said the first question of the medical section was on hepatitis. That didn't make me feel any better, but I knew my classmates had studied that section since I had it.

Third, I wanted Ray for my husband, no matter what; and my parents couldn't bribe me nor enforce their will against my stubborn streak, so they were polite and pretended they liked Ray for my sake.

Get well cards arrived daily from friends and relatives at the hospital. The biggest card came from Ray's unit signed with "Best Wishes for a Speedy Recovery" from all the guys. Mom and I made up a guest list, picked out wedding invitations from the stationery store catalog and mailed out one hundred invitations. My first wedding present was a Catholic Sick Call Set—a crucifix that opens with candles and a holy water bottle—from Connie, one of the nurses who cared for me. Later, it became a tradition to hang the crucifix gift first thing when we moved into our house, and it was the last item to leave the house when we moved out.

Sophie ordered the cake and rented the Holiday Inn for the reception. I was discharged weak, but happy, three days before the famous vows, "... *in sickness and in health till death do us part* ..."

I flew to Montana, stayed with friends, and hours later stood at the airport waiting for Ray. I was an excited mess covered in red hives that circled my neck under my high collar blouse... I had dreamed of this homecoming every day since he left on the bus one year ago. I wondered "what if" things like ... *what if Ray missed his flight?* I wanted to look calm so I clasped my hands together and stopped them from shaking.

The plane landed, the engines shut down and the door opened. We spotted each other at the same time and he ran toward me, picked me up and swung me around. He was stronger than I remembered and taller—and even more handsome. Oh God, I can't wait until Ray's all mine ... and I promise, promise, promise *only* death do us part!

August 21, 1965

Ray and I married in the Catholic Church during a Holy Mass celebrated by Monsignor Ball, who remembered Raymond from a grade school fight on the playground. After a blessing, Ray reassured Monsignor that he had changed, and they both laughed. Usually couples are married in the parish of the bride, but we did it in my college town so my classmates could attend. My parents were happy when relatives arrived in Montana from Washington and Idaho.

Nothing was fancy. The newspaper took a picture for the Sunday paper while George used his Brownie camera for a few more snapshots. Hotel music over the intercom was the background music for our reception at the Holiday Inn, and our guests gathered around tables on folding chairs. Fancy sandwiches and crackers were on a crystal plate, and spiked punch was in a bowl with matching cups. And the wedding cake was topped with a bride in white and a groom wearing a blue military uniform. Alcohol was off limits for me for a one-year period after my hepatitis. We cut the cake, fed each other a piece, tossed the bouquet and forgot about the wedding dance in our excitement.

Ray cussed when he saw the boots and tin cans attached to the bumper and whipped cream smeared on the windows in the shape of hearts. Our chivalries lasted only half a mile, because Ray hit the gas and left his buddies in the dust. He laughed about it. I opened the wedding card from my parents and held out five one-hundred dollar bills. Ray kissed the bills and waved them in front of his nose. I finally married the man of my dreams.

When we got to his parents' house to change for our honeymoon, Ray didn't have a house key. He hurried to the back yard and broke in through a bedroom window, partially covered in tacky aluminum foil that kept out the afternoon sun when his parents napped.

I slipped into my "going away suit" in the guest bedroom, the only time in my life that I wore the color rust. The smoke from Ray's cigarette trailed over his shoulder when he hosed off the car, and he put my suitcases in the trunk with his. One giant seatbelt ran across both our laps made especially for us by Ray's dad. I snuggled next to Ray. Every cell in my body was acutely aware of his electrifying presence. *"People, people needing people ..."*played on the radio. Ray switched stations.

"We don't need anyone, only each other," he said.

At first it was romantic but after driving a few more miles in silence, I disagreed.

"What about friends?" I asked.

"You don't need them either . . . *you've got me.*"

After he filled up with gas, the attendant smiled and said, *"Congratulations to the newlyweds."* We wondered how he knew. At the second station, Ray discovered a "Just Married" note

19

taped inside the gas cap. He tossed it into the can by the pump. While he paid, I retrieved it and tucked it away in my purse for our wedding book.

We made love every day of our month-long Canadian honeymoon, except on the two days we both stayed in bed with the flu. Ray read aloud passages from *The Harrad Experiment* by Robert H. Rimmer, and we got hot soup from room service. With our bodies spooned, we talked about the fatal accident at school and Ray listened with compassion. He understood how awful it was because once his friend was killed drag racing. Even though Ray believed he caused it, no one blamed him.

We pulled a small, orange U-Haul loaded with wedding presents to the new base assignment in Utah. When Ray got into unfamiliar territory, he handed me a map, but I handed it right back.

"Take it. Tell me where to go," Ray said.

"I don't know how to read it."

"Sure you do. Anyone that's finished the eighth grade can read a map."

"Well, I didn't exactly like geography class," I said.

"You should have paid attention," he tossed it back on my lap.

It went okay for quite a while, but then I had the map crooked on my lap and I told Ray to take the left fork in the road instead of the right. In the middle of nowhere, the car slid *catawampus* on the gravel road, kicked up dust, rocked, and came to a full stop. Ray pushed the door open with his arm extended, stepped out and slammed the door with such force the window rattled. He looked at me first and then pounded his fist on the hood until he made a deep indentation. I flinched. A flock of crows cawed and flapped wildly, startled by our noise on this quiet country road. Pumped with rage, Ray kicked the tires, hurt his foot and damned the world. I turned away from the windshield. *Oh God, Oh God, Oh God, help me . . . this is my husband. Oh shit. I have made a big mistake.* A shiver ascended from the small of my back.

My mother's voice echoed in my head, *"Honey, you made your bed and you can lie in it."*

I was quiet the rest of the way. I followed the blue line on the map with my finger and kept my head clear. I didn't know how to change a tire or what was under the hood of the car. No one had ever asked me to help.

When Ray got tired of driving, we stopped at a motel for the night and he was more like the nice Ray. When we arrived at our Utah destination, I thought I was most helpful when I used my own hand signals and facial expressions to help him back the trailer into a tight spot. He yelled at me to move so he could see me in his mirror. He shook his head back and forth and I could see his lips moving but couldn't hear him. Ray got out of the car and looked at the distance between the car and the building several times. I yelled back clear directions, but he wasn't very cool about it and screamed, *"Fuck!"* so I stopped helping him and didn't let him see me cry. No one had ever said *that* word around me.

Our Place & Pregnancy

We rented a small, one-bedroom, furnished, third-story apartment across from a laundromat ten miles from the Air base. Italian and oriental spices wafted down the stairwell every evening. It wasn't from my tiny kitchen because I didn't know how to cook. I kept three latches locked on the door at all times, like Ray instructed and talked through the slit to the Avon lady, a magazine sales representative and two Mormon missionaries.

Today, after Ray left for work, I tackled a recipe of my grandmother's fresh lemon pie with meringue peaks. It looked like a Betty Crocker original. Since it was the first pie I had ever made, I sampled a very small piece. Then I couldn't resist another and another until I had eaten the entire pie. When Ray returned home, he asked what I did all day. The apparent evidence, like crumbs, lemon peels or smells were missing, so I nonchalantly mentioned my soap opera, handed him the mail with a drink and hardly touched my supper.

I conceived on my honeymoon. I'm sure it was because I kept my butt elevated so the sperm reached the egg. I was so excited I called Zoe twenty minutes after I found out and shared the good news. Then I puked for the next three months, slept a lot and spent time every day at the grocery store behind our apartment building. I forgot to buy things on purpose for a reason to return the next day. I walked up and down every aisle and touched cans and packages, read all the labels and talked to the cashier.

Ray spent anywhere from three to seventeen days out of town on temporary duty. I checked newspaper ads and called around for work but hadn't found anything. When he was home, he rifled through change from my pockets and the laundromat looking for specific rare coins. This one night, I washed his military fatigues, starched and ironed them under the light of a bare bulb hanging in the bedroom, and then we had amazing sex. In the morning Ray ranted about how terrible his pants and shirt looked. He rolled them in a ball and tossed them on the closet floor. In the faint daylight, I saw the stains from the drippy starch bottle. I thought when the splotches dried they would be gone, but even the camouflages couldn't cover up the bad job. Ray grabbed another pair from the closet.

"Don't ever iron my fatigues again!" he yelled.

I stayed under the covers with my hurt feelings until the door slammed. *I'm never going to iron a damn thing for him.*

My First Job

My new employment at a private nursing home included a one-bedroom duplex with a fireplace located across the alley from the job and we moved. I had my Boards to complete to advance from graduate nurse to registered nurse with a pay raise. I reviewed my books briefly and prayed for a retentive memory because I was scared and unprepared. The lines were long, and I didn't know a soul.

After the exam began, a wave of nausea hit me like a monsoon and even slow deep breathing didn't help. I tiptoed into the bathroom accompanied by an assigned female monitor. Her presence guaranteed no cheating. My insides soured. I needed relief from the churning and the sudden pressure on my bladder and bowels. I knelt on the floor in front of a toilet and wretched back and forth like a baby hitching. I vomited with such force that my front tooth, attached to a partial plate, projected out of my mouth and floated in my undigested breakfast. I grabbed it out quickly, tucked it into my palm, and flushed the bowl. She asked to see both of my hands, and embarrassed, I slowly opened them and showed her. She handed me a towel and a glass of water, and I gargled and spit in the toilet. Then she helped me up from the floor. I washed up and returned to my desk but didn't get the last section finished before the buzzer sounded.

"Hey, you walked out with the dummies and the slowpokes," Ray said. "How did it go?"

"I'm not sure. I got sick in the middle of it." Then I cried.

Ray patted my hand. "You probably did all right. Don't worry," he said, and he fixed dinner.

Nevertheless, I was worried.

Two months later, the results arrived in the mail. I slipped the thin envelope with the Utah state emblem in the corner under my jewelry box on the dresser—the one with the ballerina that played music—because I couldn't look at it.

Thursday of the next week, I opened my letter. I sat on the edge of the bed, ran the letter opener carefully along the top of the envelope, unfolded it and stared at the numbers on the page. I read it once and then again. I reviewed the interpretation of the test grades. My hands trembled, the paper shook and my tears blurred my score. I failed a section, but I might as well have failed the whole damn exam because it meant I didn't get my license. I knelt down, beat my hands on the bed, and wailed with my mouth pressed to the mattress.

Ray stood braced in the doorway with a cigarette hanging from the corner of his mouth. "What's wrong?"

I sniffed, wiped my nose on my wrist and handed him my official test results. He left it on the dresser and opened a beer. Pizza delivery was at the door. I don't know what bothered Ray more—that I hid the results or that I failed the exam—but we didn't talk the rest of the evening. I read the newspaper and watched the television, absorbing every advertisement like there was going to be a test before retiring for the night.

When I slipped into bed, he told me that my parents wasted their money on my education and that I was a disappointment to them and to my school. Then he turned on his side and slept on the edge of the bed, while I slept sitting up, because I could hardly breathe with a plugged nose. Then my belly got this funny feeling, and at first, I had an embarrassing thought about gas, but then it suddenly happened again—I knew the baby had kicked for the first time. Since Ray thought I was stupid, I kept this joyful moment to myself.

Pregnancy wasn't an excuse, but I wasn't myself. I didn't mind the changes in my body, with bigger breasts and all that, but the mood swings made me crazy. I cried when I didn't get my way or when a picture hung crooked on the wall. I craved oranges and onion rings, got lonesome, and then bought a black and brown puppy in the pet store and named him Sloopy.

It was 11:00 p.m. when I desperately craved an egg salad sandwich. Ray offered to make me one, but I insisted it had to be store bought. After an hour of driving around, we found a day old sandwich at St. Benedict's Hospital Cafeteria. Ray tossed it through the car window and told me to eat it, but the craving had passed. I didn't want it anymore. Besides, it was wrapped so tight in saran that the egg salad squished out the sides and made the bread soggy and yellow. One look from him and I choked half of it down; the rest hit the garbage when I got home.

We attended a mandatory prenatal class. As I laid my open

palms across my abdomen and said a prayer of thanksgiving, my maternity top moved with a right jab to the ribs, and I marveled at the miracle. A few non-pregnant friends tagged along *just in case*. The uniformed instructor brought out nine jars that contained unborn fetuses in formaldehyde.

Each one floated freely in liquid, each form more developed than the last . . . all the way to term. The room buzzed when we passed them around.

~~~~

The spring Squadron picnic at Hill Air Force Base was a big annual event. I volunteered to bring a chocolate cake because I knew I couldn't screw up a box mix. But in my excitement, I opened the oven door too soon and the cake burped and caved in the middle. Because there was no time to bake another, I began the conversation in my head for the cake unveiling, tearfully wondering, *what am I going to do?* I sat on the floor with the pregnancy hormones blasting me and turned into an emotionally exhausted crybaby. Ray walked in the side door. He got down on the floor with me to see if I was okay and held me. When I showed him my cake, he laughed and then apologized and kissed me.

Unpredictably, Ray hurried to the little corner store and bought an Easter Bunny in a nest. He plunked it into the hole in the center of the cake and blended the chocolate frosting. We walked into the picnic grounds proud of our contribution and our secret became the centerpiece of potluck. He's my hero again — Ray's my man.

The GIs drank booze and bullshitted with one another. I didn't smoke cigarettes during my pregnancy, but I'd sit next to Ray and tell him to blow the rings at me. Back then it was perfectly acceptable to inhale and exhale like I had learned in college. We all did it. I didn't drink either. Instead, I sat on top of an uncovered picnic table and watched kids play. After two hours of chatting and sitting in the sun, I was nauseated and pale with beads of sweat. I moved under the shade of a tree, drank lemonade, and insisted on leaving.

"Damn," he said. "I hate to leave. The party is just getting started."

The next day my doctor scolded me and confined me to bed. Ray slathered sticky creams over my blistered arms and legs for a week while I lie naked, my growing belly covered with a receiving blanket like a flag draped over a coffin. And that's when I began to worry whether my baby would be okay . . . have all its fingers and toes and be normal, and I began to pray more.

The white crib covered with lamb decals tucked nicely in the corner of our bedroom. It was a gift from one of the families in his unit. I thanked them graciously with hugs. Ray later said now we owed them. Our baby carrier was brand new. It sat in the back of the closet next to Ray's shoes, lined against the wall. I had two maternity dresses. The dressy one from my mother-in-law was blue, with a white Peter Pan collar. My other one was black. I only liked the black one.

Our New Addition

Lost in Space was on television when, with an astounding contraction, my labor started. Forty minutes later another came like a charley horse in my belly and then at thirty minutes, during *Sea Hunt*. When they were a jolting twenty minutes apart and stronger, I called the base for instructions. We left the house when Johnny Carson finished his last interview. On the way, my belly tightened into a hard ball, so I blew out my air and concentrated on my imperfect breath. It was difficult holding back my sighs; but I handled it because I promised Ray, who kept score, I'd make him proud of me; and besides, I owed him one for being the "cake savior."

"You're still the same," the nurse said after my examination. "You haven't dilated since your office visit this morning, so you can go home now, Emma."

"No, it's one in the morning. I'm gonna have a baby right

here, tonight, and not in my car."

After I got my way and settled into a bed, both of my legs shot straight out from the force of the amniotic fluid. When it splashed up the wall, Ray grabbed towels, covered the puddle and apologized for the mess.

The nurse laughed and tossed more towels onto the bed. "It's okay . . . Not to worry," she said.

I drifted off lightly after an injection. I didn't want to kiss Ray, look at him, or listen to his dumb jokes. I was exhausted, so the nurse insisted Ray leave so I could rest; and she told him with some authority that it would be morning before I delivered. He said he'd check on the dog, but as soon as he walked in our house, he was called back because I was in full labor.

The doctor pulled a scrub gown over his tee shirt and plaid Bermuda shorts at 3:00 a.m. Ray arrived out of breath and pressed his face against the oval window until the doctor waved him in. He shoved his long arms into a scrub gown and masked up. *I wished Ray was a doctor. He looked good in scrubs.* They both stood at the end of the table and discussed football, while I tried to push a baby bigger than that out my bottom. My baby butted itself against a thick wall of skin trying to exit into this world. That continued until the doctor rotated the baby. By that time, I was too tired to push. The sweet relief of ice chips spooned into my cottonmouth was an oasis. That was followed by the sound of a scissor blade but I didn't feel a thing. The room cheered for the last big push. I did it. It was the best.

හ

It was 3:20 a.m. on Wednesday, June 15, 1966. I had my baby girl: 8 pounds, 1 ounce and 21 inches long. My Tori was perfect. Ray winked at me, called her *his princess* and rushed off to find a telephone to tell the grandparents. After stitches, a nurse took Tori into the nursery and pushed my bed through the big double doors into the twelve-bed maternity ward. I was in the corner.

The maternity ward allowed only mothers. The fathers had to stand outside in the hall in front of the nursery windows and wait for moms to come out into the hallway.

Four hours later, as I was having the best dreamless sleep of my entire life, a three hundred pound woman in uniform came into the room, yanked open the white canvas curtains that separated each of us and screamed, "Hit the showers, ladies!"

I shockingly joined the others in a gang shower where I saw for the first time a group of naked women with wrinkled bellies and full breasts. I didn't take my eyes off the floor. She screamed orders and we made our beds, took the lamps from the head of the bed, spread our legs and placed the bulb square in front of the stitches for twenty minutes. I was the youngest "first time mother" in the ward, and no one was friendly. I attempted conversations when I collected all their bones from dinner for my dog. But they acted like they didn't like me.

I handed the bag of bones to Ray when he visited. We stood in the hallway along with the other parents and waited for the curtains to open. We positioned ourselves front and center of the nursery window for the best view, waved at Tori, cooed and smiled. Her pink cheeks and button nose looked like my side of the family. We all acted so goofy.

"Oh no. She's crying. What's wrong?"

"She's hungry," Ray said and put his arm around my shoulder. I wondered how he knew that. Then time was up and visiting hours were over. In the maternity ward, I held Tori once every three hours for twenty minutes. I gave her a bottle of formula and she fell asleep in my arms and looked like a cherub. Ray didn't want me to breast feed her because he said it would ruin the shape of my perky breasts. This decision would end up being something I'd always regret. I didn't even question him back then because, at the time, it wasn't fashionable for the military moms to nurse. Each visit I examined every inch of her soft skin and prayed to be a good mother. If I was in a room by myself, I would have sung to her, but not when the others could hear me.

My parents arrived for a visit with my sister and Peter, the French poodle. They were proud of me and told me so. I put on a great act for them while they were there for three days and they thought I was doing well. Mom said to call if I needed anything, but I didn't want her to know that I didn't know what I was doing.

When Tori was eleven days old and she wouldn't stop crying, Ray screamed at me to make her be quiet. I was sleep deprived, my stitches itched and my tailbone was sprained. I sat in pain on a rubber ring covered with a pillowcase and never imagined this scenario.

"I said make her stop crying, dammit," Ray yelled.

"*Okay!*" I screamed back.

I closed the bedroom door and quick-stepped into the living room with Tori. I flipped through my OB textbook, jiggling her on my hip. Ray told me I should naturally know about babies, being a woman, but hell, I didn't even babysit. I rocked her to soft music, sang and swaddled her in a bunny wrap. Then I begged and pressed my lips to her ear and chanted, "Please, please, please, please," like a mantra, for five full minutes. Finally, Tori slept, her hand tightly grasped around my little finger. Her belly rose and fell with even, regular, deep breaths. I closed my swollen eyelids, knowing I'd die if anything bad happened to her. I admitted to myself I didn't know what I was doing most of the time, but I hated being reminded. I was smart, had common sense and was determined to be the best mother.

Viet Nam/Thailand Tour

I returned home and lived with my parents while Ray completed a one-year tour of duty in Thailand flying missions over Viet Nam. Tori, Sloopy and I slept in my brother's bedroom in the finished basement. I cried at night, rocked my Tori for hours, and repeatedly sang the same song: "*If it takes forever, I will wait for you . . .*" And at night the dog slept stretched along my backside.

And when Walt Disney died and I thought my baby would never be able to know about him, I cried. Pop-tops appeared on cans of soda and beer, and I laughed with joy.

I wrote letters every day on filmy airmail paper to an APO address in New York. I was bored with television and sad and lonesome without a husband, so I spent time preparing weekly care packages filled with popcorn, cookies, candy and paperbacks for Ray. For a laugh, I put a real look-alike gray rubber mouse in the bottom of a care package and imagined his laughter, but it backfired and he scolded me in his next letter.

Each night, I watched the news and kept track of the body count. Bob Hope entertained the troops—I sat on the floor next to the television and looked for Ray in the audience. My dad said to back up from the screen or I'd ruin my eyes. But mostly I was looking for Ray. I was forgetting what Ray looked like. I mean, I remembered his crooked nose, his square shaped ears and his blue eyes, but those pieces together wouldn't make his face. The soldiers on TV smiled and laughed. It looked like they were having fun. I wasn't having fun. The GIs cheered especially loud when Rachel Welch came on stage. *Wow, I'd like to look like her . . . but what would it matter*?

My parents were old fashioned, protective and strict—they would not let me go anywhere.

"You're a married woman and you'll stay home and behave yourself."

"But Mom, Dad! The party is only two houses away. It's New Year's Eve, for crying out loud!"

"We said *no!*"

I was unhappy and struck up a deal with my mom and dad to go visit Ray's parents for a week. I packed up a couple of bags. Sophie and George were so happy we came; we stayed for the remaining six months. The house belonged to me while they were at work. I cooked dinner, straightened up and washed clothes. George and Sophie drank everyday and they didn't mind if I made rounds with a girlfriend on Wednesday nights.

I put Tori to bed and Sloopy hunkered down with their dog by the front door. My girlfriend and I stood in line at "Gramma's," a local bar with a live band, toilet seats, and framed black and white photos of hundreds of real granny faces. The stage was a big brass bed, the music was rock and roll, and the wild dancing and insincere laughter helped me forget my loneliness.

Early one evening after I put Tori to bed, I thought I heard my mother-in-law calling me from the bedroom. I tapped first and opened their door. *Omigod,* they were having noisy sex! I shut the door quickly and stepped into the bathroom, wanting to flush myself down the toilet. Their bed banged against the bathroom wall and I hurried back out to the living room and turned up the television. One hour later, George, smothered in aftershave, sauntered through the living room, whistling. He got ice from the kitchen and headed back to their bedroom. We didn't speak. This unforgettable incident was wood burned in my mind.

80

Finally, the big day arrived when Ray was coming home. I wore his favorite dress and pearls hoping to cover the hives on my neck from my nerves. The sun reflected off the silver plane, and I leaned against the gates, while my hand cupped my eyes. Ray, handsome in his military dress blues, paused when he stepped off the plane. He looked around and I was unable to contain myself; I cried out his name not taking my eyes off the face I longed to hold. We ran toward each other in what felt like slow motion, and when he kissed me, it was like the movies. Now all the parts of his face were there and I examined him like a new mother examines her baby.

During Ray's one-month leave before his assignment in Germany, we visited family, attended parties and said our good-byes. Tori and I were to follow Ray on a commercial flight to Frankfurt. I was scared because after we completed the dental requirements, and right before the flight, we both felt sick. No one helped me and things got worse. We ran temperatures of 104 degrees and got the flu, but Ray assured me we would do fine—and I believed him because he said so. He was an *expert* at convincing me that I could do whatever he wanted me to do.

For the last time, I covered the sandbox, hugged the dog, checked under the beds and made sure my passport was handy. My bag weighed the recommended sixty-six pounds, and Tori's chubby hand held tightly to the wooden handle on her cardboard suitcase. And no one would suspect the box with a picture of a little lamb and pink clouds contained her daddy's heavy camera and lens. When we drove away, Sloopy got out of the gate and chased us down the middle of the street. The wind plastered her long feathered black ears to her head while her tongue slapped her leather lips. I watched her until we were out of sight because somehow I knew I would never see her again.

Our New Home in Germany

Tori and I had a six-hour layover in New York's Kennedy Airport. Sloopy's dog leash hooked perfectly into Tori's belt loop. Several people at the counter wanted to know where to purchase such a harness, and when I explained it belonged to our dog we left behind, they thought the idea brilliant.

Tori sat on my lap in her green wool hat, long coat and lined snow pants, and her pink face and freckled nose glistened with sweat. Then a dark-skinned woman with an oozing small pox scab sat down next to us, smiled at Tori and spoke in a foreign language to the man with her. The thought of a kidnapping entered my tired mind, and I picked up all our belongings and moved quickly to the bathroom where we hid on a big couch and opened snacks from a vending machine. We stuck close together, ate and napped until our TWA flight number came over the intercom.

Tori wore a little flight pin on her clothes given to her by the flight attendant. We played quiet games, colored and put puzzles together between our meals. From the air, the German countryside looked familiar, like stateside—open areas of quilt-like patches in varying shades of green, brown and yellow. After twelve hours of being airborne, Tori fell asleep upon landing in Frankfurt.

Ray met us in a compact, gray, Opel station wagon. He talked excitedly for the next forty-five minutes about his job, our house and how we'd adjust quickly because he'd tell us what to do. Our home was a lovely two-bedroom, furnished, apartment, fifteen miles from the base on the edge of town. When we arrived, we parked in the driveway and entered through a big double front door. Then up the stairs to the left was our apartment directly above the landlord's unit. Ray hugged us both and poured himself a cognac before starting the tour.

All of the modern rooms were off a long hallway with blonde hardwood floors. The bedrooms were without closets. The doors had no round doorknobs, only levers. There were no faucets in the kitchen, only a two-gallon glass jar attached to the wall above the sink. When you pushed the little black button, the sink filled with water and if you pushed the red button, it heated the water for the dishes. In the bathroom, a suspended chain flushed the toilet. Outside, all of the windows were wooden air raid slats that blocked out even a crack of light.

Our German proprietors, Ernst and Sieglinda, lived downstairs with two daughters. Even though both of us were of German heritage, my father had recently informed me that *"oma"* was grandma and *"opa* "was grandpa. Everything was foreign here, including our marriage. Ray said he would give exact instructions on how I should act.

After we put Tori to bed, Ray stirred his drink with his finger, opened a bottle of beer for me and insisted I had to learn to handle my alcohol—build up tolerance so I wouldn't embarrass him. Since the label said this beer contained vitamin C, I agreed to add a beer each day until the weekend party in the local pub. On my first night in a foreign country, I hit the bed exhausted, happy and much too tipsy to make love.

I was ready—my long hair flipped in the latest fashion, my eyes circled in dark eyeliner, and lots of skin showing between my mini skirt and black shiny high heel boots. Ray liked what he saw and introduced me to his buddies, who raised their eyebrows, elbowed each other and made soft wolf whistles. I bit the inside of my cheek and looked away. When everyone arrived, a tall glass boot filled with beer passed hand to hand, from one person to the next. In order to drink from this boot, one must know exactly how to tilt the glass to avoid being literally sloshed with the entire contents. My few days of practice at home paid off and I was officially accepted.

Helde, the owner of the bar, brought out her own special homemade schnapps and made a toast, *"Welcome Ray's hausfrau!"* she yelled with her glass raised in my direction.

The liquor slid down my throat like sweet juice until my head was spinning, my stomach was flipping and my face was on fire. "Tom Dooley" blared from the jukebox in German. It had never occurred to me that someone listened to *our* music in *their* own language.

Ray ignored my signals to leave, so I pushed my way past three GIs coming in the door, hung my head in the shadows and puked in the parking lot. I heard muted sounds of snickering and laughter behind me and hoped, whomever they were, that they didn't know Ray. I waited in the car. He yelled his good-byes, got into the car and didn't say a word—no need to say anything. Part of me was ashamed of myself, but the other part laughed about all the *wasted* practice beers. Too late now; I'd already disappointed him. And the truth was that I could not handle my booze, and he couldn't handle life without it.

~~~~

My parents told me I could call them collect from Germany any time I wanted to, so every week I caught Mom up on the latest. Then the rules changed. My dad said to call once a month and three minutes was the limit. There was never enough time to find out how they were doing other than the standard answer, *"We're fine."*

I hung notes on the wall by the telephone and talked faster. I wanted to tell them what happened after Mass—that time when we greeted the priest on our way out and then Tori cried all the way home because she didn't get to shake hands with God. And I wanted to tell them she ran for her big, wooden rosary when I asked her, *"Where are your knuckles?"* and that I cried, because all day long, I played with Tori and had no adult woman friends.

"Write more letters . . ." they said, and hung up.

I needed to get a grown-up's life.

A group of women from the NCO Wives Club traveled by bus to the Tulip Festival and lunch in Holland on Mother's Day for fifteen dollars. But the day before this spectacular excursion, Tori clung to me, cried, fussed and rubbed her tummy. Her swollen neck was a give away, but then small pustules appeared on her belly that made a very sick combination of mumps and chickenpox! I slathered Tori in calamine lotion, covered her hands with clean socks and hid her *"chicken pops,"* as she called them, so she wouldn't scratch. Ray told me to go anyway, but I could not leave her side, and on this Mother's Day, I was like a real mother.

The NCO Wives Club Welcoming

Once a week, I routinely took Tori to the base nursery while I shopped. Today I dropped her off and attended a luncheon at the NCO Wives Club so I could meet other women. When I got inside the lobby, I deliberately eased past the slot machines toward the bathroom. I nearly knocked over a short, stocky woman while glancing at the elections poster on the door. Her almond shaped nails matched her deep raspberry lipstick, a brown bobby pin held down a dark runaway curl on the top of her head, and her wide hips wobbled unevenly when she exited. And I sneezed.

"Gesundheit," she said.

"Thank you," I replied. Hey, I already know *one* German word, I thought.

"I'm Anne," she said and pumped my hand like a politician before she left the bathroom.

At the card table, I signed the guest book, got a nametag and was invited to sit with them when the program started. We toasted glasses of spiked punch and enjoyed a lovely luncheon with linen tablecloths, a French cafe' decor and entertainment from a barbershop quartet.

One of the women suggested that I run for an office and meet even more people. I shrugged my shoulders and said "Okay." I was game, especially when they all cheered me on.

During the announcements, my name was added to the ballot on the blank line below the unopposed President. (Unbeknownst to me, they wanted to get rid of her.) I stood when my name was called, smiled and gave a little *queen wave*. I had no idea what this club did, but I was having fun. Then Anne reared up, the unopposed President with the raspberry lips, and waved at me across the room. I shook my head and smiled back at her.

I won by *one* vote. They recounted all the ballots. We drank a little more, made toasts to Anne for all her hard work, and thanked her. She was gracious and a supportive loser.

"Did you vote for yourself?" Ray asked.

"Well, yes. Aren't you supposed to?"

"That's the only reason you won, you know."

"Ooooh! I guess you're right, but it seems stupid to run for an office and *not* vote for yourself!"

"So you actually think you'll pull this presidency gig off?" he said.

"Of course," I responded with a new confidence from both the spiked punch and woman friends, whose votes boosted me in a way that Ray would not understand. "I picked Anne for my Parliamentarian, which was a very smart move on my part. She will sit beside me at all functions and answer my questions. I know I can't do it without her, Ray, but I'm a fast learner and she's happy for me. So, get ready, *Mister President*, because next week, we sit at the head table with the base Commander."

Strike One

My chin quivered and I held back the tears. There were no locks on the doors and Ray followed me all over the house, in and out of the rooms, mimicking my face and my footsteps.

"Stop!" I begged. "Stop it Ray!"

He was right behind me up until his loud, hard laugh turned into a smoker's coughing spell, which gave me the only chance I had to slip away. I ran down the hall, closed the bedroom door, leaned against it, and braced my foot. Only seconds later, he pounded his fists hard against the wood.

"You think you got away from me?"

"Leave . . . me . . . alone!" I screamed.

"What's the matter with you?" he asked in a hoarse voice.

"I . . . want. . . to be. . . alone. That's all."

Ray pulled the lever and shoved so hard, I slid backwards in my socks across the hardwood as the door opened. He grabbed me around the waist. He tickled me and it hurt when he dug his fingers into my ribs. Then without thinking, a switch flipped in my brain and I brought my right arm over my head and hit him in the chest with as much force as I could. All 217 pounds of him dropped to the floor without hesitation, like a sack, in a heap. He was out cold. I was terrified and pictured myself in stripes—in prison for murder. My temples throbbed and I was nearly out of breath when I knelt beside him.

"Ray, Ray . . ." I unbuttoned his shirt collar, raised his head up and cradled him. I kissed his forehead, his ear, his nose and his forehead again.

"Shit lady. You coulda killed me," he said surprised.

"I'm sorry. I'm so sorry."

Then I helped him up and pushed him onto the bed. We

barely spoke the rest of the evening. I was scared—what if he died because I slugged him? He said, "Go to sleep."

I lay beside him and watched his chest go up and down. I counted his hot breaths and the seconds between them. His soft snores calmed me. And, I prayed and watched for three more nights. *God have mercy* . . . and then I got it—I understood murder!

Everyone has a breaking point.

The Accident

Early one morning, a cobalt blue BMW *Glas* sports car pulled up in our driveway. I peeked through the sheer curtains and Ray popped his head out the passenger window and waved.

"Ray?"

"We're taking a test drive!" he yelled.

Ray wrinkled his nose at Tori, who giggled when we climbed into the car. She had changed clothes three times and had my pearls around her neck. In her pocket, she carried a handful of plastic butterfly barrettes and a *Pfennig*.

"Hans will drive first and then it's my turn," Ray said.

In the back seat, straps dangled from the ceiling. I put one hand through the leather loop and the other around Tori and pulled her close. The dash was a dark brown, varnished wood grain and it smelled expensive. "Hold on tight," he warned fastening a lap belt. "This baby really kicks." And Tori hugged her knees over her little plaid dress.

We flew on the straight road through the forest for two miles. Then Hans darted back and forth on the switchbacks, handling the car like a professional. We dipped into a valley and nearly met ourselves on a hairpin curve. My heart pounded hard against Tori's small back, from both the excitement and terror, because I had never gone that fast before.

When they switched places, Ray's devilish grin reflected in the rear view mirror. Evidently, the thrill of racing was still in his blood. He chuckled and contorted his mouth. His hands tightened on the steering wheel. At first Ray had controlled his speed in the corners, but on the straightaway, he cut loose. Our bodies pressed hard against the leather seats, and then over against the window, and then back against the leather—like a carnival ride. I begged St. Christopher for protection for us, from us, and feared for our lives as I watched a stranger.

We returned to the dealership and Ray was giddy. By midday, we had purchased this BMW *Glas*. I'd never seen him so excited and it began to rub off on me. I wanted to phone my parents and tell them, but I had to wait until the end of the month.

I had never expected to call my parents about a fatal accident.

The accident happened off base. We attended a late-afternoon party at a Tech Sergeant's home after we took Tori to the base nursery. The music blared from huge speakers next to the reel-to-reel tape deck. Our new BMW was the topic of conversation. At first it reminded me of high school with the boys in one corner and the girls in the other. However, here the men smoked cigarettes, mixed drinks and started the barbeque outside, while the women gathered in the kitchen and discussed husbands and children. I envied the one couple in the living room dancing.

After the picnic dinner and several drinks, we played games. All the greased-up men flirted with the women. First, there was a race where we passed the raw egg under your chin to the person behind you, then "Twister," and I got so tangled I fell on my face. Then, lastly, a game some drunk made up. We gathered in a circle, pulled a bedroom sheet taut and blew a cotton ball around with the goal being: don't let it touch you or you're out.

When it was time to get Tori from the base nursery, Rolland, the newest and youngest airman in the unit, asked Ray if he could ride in our BMW. Ray put his arm around him like a big brother and told him to come along while he picked up Tori.

I sunk. I was ready to go home. Glaring daggers at Ray didn't work. "Last call" meant *give me a double* and it sat on the coffee table for when he returned. I hated being the last ones to leave a party. Ray kissed me quick and rushed out the door. I waved at the back of his head. He peeled out of the yard, and I tossed my sweater on a chair and headed out to the kitchen for yet another cup of coffee.

It had been twenty minutes since Ray had gone to pick up Tori, and I wondered what took so long. When the phone rang, I put my coffee cup down, shot past the host and grabbed it, even though it wasn't my house.

"Hello. Yes, this is Emma. Ray left fifteen minutes ago. I'll be there. I'm sorry . . . Thank you."

I heard the sirens and my chest tightened as the sound grew closer. I ran screaming into the yard, "Oh my god, look!" Across the field, in the darkest of nights, red and yellow lights spun like haunting shadows across the sky. The music stopped. "There's been an accident. *Someone please . . . please take me to the nursery.*"

Down the stretch of highway, about a mile from the house, the ambulance, fire truck and emergency vehicles blocked the road in full view of a blue BMW flipped on its back in the ditch with one door ajar. The tires smoked and the smell of gasoline permeated the thick air. A shiver ran across my shoulders and down my arms, and I hurried toward the ambulance.

"Ma'am, get back," ordered the Military Police waving a bully stick.

The body under the sheet had red matted hair, the face covered. I stood on my tiptoes and the MP lifted a pair of shattered, black, horn-rimmed glasses from the mud in the tire rut. He placed them on the gurney and waved the ambulance around the debris strewn across the country road. It was the new kid: *What's-his-name?* Ron *something*—the one that wanted to ride along.

I spotted Ray clear on the other side of the road. Overhead lights illuminated the pitch-black night. He was wandering in the field holding his arm across his chest cursing. Ray bent down, dug in the dirt, coughed hard and spat blood.

"*Son-of-a-bitch*! What happened? Where is Rolland?"

The medic ordered Ray to sit down and slipped a triangular sling over his right shoulder.

"Is Rolland gone? Is Rolland gone?" Ray yelled. "Someone talk to me, dammit!"

"Yes, Ray. They had to get him to the hospital first," I answered.

"*Ma'am*," he ordered, "you *have* to leave . . . NOW!"

Our friend, Jess, put his arm around my stiff shoulders and opened the door of his car. I dropped into the seat. He patted my hand. I was unable to make sense of the last few minutes, and all I could smell was gasoline and burnt rubber.

"Wake me from this nightmare, Jess."

"I'd like to, but it's real bad for Ray. He's up for Tech Sergeant and outranks the new airmen. No matter what happens, he's responsible."

And the new kid? I closed my eyes to think better. *Omigod, that new kid is dead.*

We drove in silence. The shrieking sirens passed us as we headed off in the opposite direction.

Jess brought Tori out to the car and put her on my lap.

"Where's Daddy?" she asked in a sleepy voice.

"Shh! Go back to sleep, Tori."

"Mommy, you didn't come and get me."

"I'm sorry, baby."

"Everybody left."

I pulled her in closer and kissed the part separating her pigtails. A few minutes later she started in again. "Where's Daddy?"

"He's on base tonight."

"Lady is mad at you," said Tori.

"What lady?" I asked.

"The one that said '*Stop crying like a baby.*' I don't like her."

"I'm sorry. It's okay now. Mommy is here and we're going home."

"But I want Daddy."

It was two in the morning. I couldn't sleep. It was only dinnertime in the States. I called my parents. Both of them were home and each picked up a phone. I was so relieved when I heard their voices that I began to sob. I told them about the accident and Ray being in the hospital. Then I remembered they didn't even like Ray. They *tolerated* him. My father cussed, and I regretfully remembered his long-ago bargain that if I didn't marry Ray, he would send me to San Francisco to live and work with his sister, my Aunt Ginny, a Nurse Supervisor at Mercy.

"Well, are you okay?" my father asked.

"Yes, I'm fine, except . . ."

"Well, we're hanging up then. Get some rest."

When it clicked, I looked at the receiver. "Hello? Mom?" She didn't answer and the dangling tangled line was like a severed umbilical cord. I hung up puzzled, sat on the edge of my bed and wondered how to handle things like an adult. Still fully dressed, I pulled the covers over my head, curled up into the fetal position and cried.

The Investigation

I stood in the hallway outside Ray's room at the base hospital. An officer standing at the foot of his bed conducted an investigation of the accident. Ray looked straight ahead with lifeless eyes— emotionless—until he spotted me through the glass door and gave a small "go away" wave. Ray told the officer that Rolland was the driver, he wouldn't slow down, and that Rolland lost control of the car—and that's when they rolled.

The driver was Rolland. Why did he say that?

I wanted to protect Ray, but it didn't sound right; and besides, when they left the house, I swear, I saw Ray get behind the wheel. I tried to picture the switch, but I knew in my gut that Ray wouldn't have allowed a stranger to drive his car because I had not even been allowed to drive yet.

The officer walked toward me, nodded politely with a deeply observant gaze, stepped back from the door, pulled the blinds and told me to wait until he finished. Then a Staff Sergeant from the Coroner's office approached and asked for my help to clear up something—the identification of an item found at the scene.

Please don't ask me any questions like how much anyone drank or if Ray has ever been in an accident before. What happens if I say the wrong thing?

He showed me into the small room next to the nurse's station that was cold and bare with no pictures on the wall, one gray table, two straight-back chairs and a large mirror. He pulled out my chair, opened a box and placed two men's Seiko stainless steel watches at my fingertips for my examination.

"Take your time," he said.

The watch faces looked similar with lighted backgrounds, glow-in-the-dark hands and calendars that displayed the day of the week. Funny, I never paid much attention to Ray's watch. *What kind of a wife am I?* But I knew the shape of the freckles on his wrist and the sound the clasp made when he took it off at night. The Staff Sergeant had a kind, compassionate face. He watched me examine first one, then the other, and sigh, glancing back at the first one.

"Would you like some water?"

My mouth was dry, but I shook my head no and glanced down at my Timex. I wondered if he'd pick mine out of a line up. I pointed to the second one and rationalized, in my confused state of mind, that the watch that ran must belong to the heart that still beat.

"Thank you," he said. "I'll send this other one with the personal effects . . ."

It was later that I discovered why Ray never again wore his watch—I had selected the wrong one.

When Dr. Kelleher made rounds, he discontinued Ray's IV, removed the needle from his bruised inner arm and asked me to hand him a Band-Aid. When the doctor removed the stethoscope from his neck and listened to Ray's chest, without thinking, I reached up, untied the knot on the back of Ray's hospital gown and assisted Dr. Kelleher. He placed the circular piece on his hairy back, listened for breath sounds, and pulled the chest tube. Then he rewrapped the wide ace bandages that supported the broken ribs.

"Ray, I want you to stop smoking—at least for now," said Dr. Kelleher. "And I may as well ask this in front of your wife," he continued. "Will you change your story about the way the accident happened . . . for the record?"

"No sir," Ray said without flinching.

"Please, say exactly what happened," I begged softly, resisting the temptation to scream at him.

Dr. Kelleher gently, but *very* matter-of-fact-like, explained the Military Police concluded Rolland died on impact when thrown from the vehicle, and Ray's type of chest injury was the result of blunt force trauma from the steering wheel.

Ray's sober expression never changed.

Tech Sergeant Jesse, from his unit, entered the room and corroborated the story, adding more fuel. "The radio tower on the flight line, parallel to the road where the accident occurred, reported a low-flying aircraft at 11:05 p.m. Ray, it was *your* BMW going at extreme speed."

"Look," Ray said shrugging his shoulders. "A guy is dead—I outrank him. Therefore, I'm responsible, no matter what."

"But Ray . . . *the doctor said* . . ."

"I told you," he interrupted, "I don't want a confession on my record."

"Ray . . ."

"No!" he yelled. "I said NO!"

My heart closed. I ordered lunch but I don't remember eating. The food was gone from my plate, but I was still hungry. My mother's voice lived somewhere in my head and kept saying, "*If someone lies . . . they cheat and steal.*" I thought Ray was so smart, but today I changed my mind.

How could my mother know this? I wished she was wrong this once.

~~~~

The Master Sergeant escorted Rolland's body to his home state of California. He had the gruesome task of telling his parents that their only child was a victim of a single rollover accident—not even a military hero. The Air Force Commander charged Ray with vehicular manslaughter, demoted him to an Airman First Class, and took his license away for one year. I was grateful Ray wasn't charged with vehicular homicide with a "dishonorable discharge." He was lucky. But he didn't act like it.

It was humiliating when Ray was busted, but it didn't make any difference to him. Ray stayed Ray. He still used Tabasco on his eggs, drank cognac, and smoked Marlboro cigarettes. His friends came over to the house, colored in Tori's coloring book, and built Lego houses on our coffee table with her. I kept my discomfort to myself and drove Ray to and from work, to the doctors and anywhere he wanted to go. Ray thanked me for rides. He kissed me good-bye. He kissed me hello.

Jackpot

Ray took a job bartending at the NCO club to make some extra money to pay off debts. He played the slots during his breaks and often caught a ride home after his shift. Occasionally he'd be tipsy, but one night Ray called my name from the doorway and nudged me. I was in a deep sleep, so he switched the overhead light on and off, on and off and yelled "JACKPOT!"

Startled, I opened my eyes and sat up. Ray closed the door and tossed green paper straight up into the air with both hands. Four hundred one-dollar bills landed on the bed and in my hair. He spun around proudly like a ballerina. We kissed, laughed, and hugged. We counted it and made piles of twenties, and then it was my turn. I threw the stacks into the air, but softer now, so we wouldn't wake Tori. The celebration was exhilarating and surprisingly erotic. We made love until we were exhausted while hot tears streaked down my face—a profound relief from my loneliness. The only time I belonged or mattered was when Ray made love to me. He would never understand because I couldn't explain or understand it myself.

Ray reached for the flattened soft pack of cigarettes. He lit one and handed it to me. I sucked deeply on it and exhaled several little "O-rings" with my lips, passing it back to his impatient mouth. When he turned away from me without words, I tucked my knees under his butt and pressed my breasts into his back. I lived for these moments and didn't want to go to sleep—to lose that feeling. This was why I stayed with him because, right when I wanted to bail out, something like this would happen, where I imagined I was like every loved woman in a movie scene. He always ruined my escape. Those unpredictable chunks of affection refueled every fresh start, and that was how it was.

The next morning, cheeks pink from the pressure of Ray's whiskers, I made breakfast: soft-boiled eggs, dark toast, jam and black coffee. Tori was asleep. Ray didn't talk, and I quietly held onto the last speck of last night's passion. The calmness in this silence was welcome.

After breakfast, I cleaned the kitchen and Ray tucked himself behind me at the sink. He trapped his leg between both of mine and moved slowly. His warm breath tickled the nape of my neck. He whispered," Let's *spend* the money." Ray's kiss was a passionate promissory note we'd make love again—not now, but soon. He was irresistible. Instead of making the past due car payments for the totaled car and the Opel buy-back, we headed straight for the music store and blew all the money on a *Grundig* stereo sound system.

Ray carried the equipment upstairs to our apartment and lifted each piece out of the box. He read the directions quietly aloud. I watched from the couch. "Make yourself useful and pour me a drink," he said.

It was no surprise, being an expert in the electronics field, when the stereo system setup was perfect. Whatever he did, he did well. The tall, maple speakers matched our coffee table and fit each corner of the room.

When Ray finished a job, he had this ritual. First, he ran his fingers back through his thick hair, and then he straightened his trousers around his waist and tucked in his shirttail. I perused the records looking for the perfect one to initiate his winnings, but he found it first. Johnny Ray bellowed out "Cry" and I got goose bumps, wanted to dance, make love or celebrate in Ray's arms, but he sat in the overstuffed chair, rolled his sleeves up over his elbows, lit up, and sipped his cognac with his eyes closed, his chin tilted upward, in his own world, as if gloating.

Hippies

I delighted in the man I *thought* I married; but within hours, remembered I was only his showpiece, and he wasn't what I had imagined either. Ray chose my clothes and asked my friends to show me how to apply make up. His facial expressions gave away whether my dresses, skirts, and sweaters met his approval, which I wore only because he liked me that way. I didn't own any long pants, slacks, or jeans because he hated seeing women in pants. But Ray never left the house without kissing us good-bye and making eye contact, taking one good last look in case, well perhaps, just what if mysteriously, he never came back. And each exit left me wondering when I would see him again.

Late in the fall, on a chilly, boring afternoon, while Ray was off to another base on temporary duty, I stared at the pictures in the *Stars and Stripes* newspaper for the longest time. The headlines read, "Hippies Cause a Peaceful Ruckus in San Francisco." Even though those two words didn't belong together, I wanted to be a hippie in the middle of the streets in San Francisco, liberated, doing this peace-and-love thing amidst my friends. I missed them.

When Tori woke up, I put blossoms in our hair, and we painted large sunflowers on our dresses. I swung my bra over my head, tossed it through the air, and she laughed and tossed a monkey doll. We danced in circles in our bare feet on the hardwood floors, scooted up and down the hallway until we were out of breath. Tori hopped on one leg and twirled until she fell down on the blanket she dragged behind her. She laughed so hard her eyes shut to slits. We played for hours. Between naps and meals, I read paperbacks and watched the German television commercials that only aired for one hour early in the evening before the regularly broadcast programs.

Each evening Tori padded off to bed after the television *Sandmannchen* told a story and sang a good night song. She lined all the little rubber sand man dolls on the floor in front of the TV while we sang with the Sand Man and waved as each little doll said good night to her. When I tucked her in and kissed her, she wrapped her arms tight around my neck and giggled. I pretended I couldn't get away for just a moment and then closed her door.

My Heartaches

I was six months pregnant and barely showing when Dr. Hill, a new obstetrician to the office, stood beside the exam table and said he was sorry but my baby had no audible heartbeat. He looked away, patted my knee over the drape covering my legs and left me shivering in a thin gown.

My eyes followed him out of the room. *You're a mean doctor. I don't believe you. Last week you were the dermatologist. What do you know about babies?* These thoughts I kept to myself, even though they screamed at me to become words and fight. When the door closed, I stared at the nurse who looked away when she gave me my clothes.

"Please listen one more time," I begged.

Her pitiful expression didn't change, but she gave me her stethoscope. I moved it around on my belly in several places hunting, searching for life. I sat quietly stared intently at the hands of the clock on the wall and waited for a flutter—anything. There was no heartbeat. There was no movement.

"Can I see Dr. Mann? He knows me." I fought back the tears.

"That can be arranged . . . when you come back next week dear." The nurse told me that military law said I had to carry my fetus until the physician was positively sure that no life existed for the unborn.

Each day passed, leaving me more hopeless than the day before. A week later, I sat in the waiting room with chatty expectant mothers-to-be and held a magazine in front of my face so I wouldn't have to talk to anyone. I was the mother of a dead baby, and the secret I carried was crazy difficult. I plodded up to the desk for the next three weeks for, what I called, "my fake appointments," each time wanting to run. Keeping them kept Ray's unit and Tori from knowing our sadness at least for a while longer.

Very early the next morning, after my last appointment, I knew that something was wrong. I woke up soaked; I moaned from the cramps and rolled over. Ray opened one eye and yawned. "What's the matter?" he said.

"I think it's over; but don't look. Stay on your side—I'm a mess."

Ray got up, toddled into the bathroom and washed the blood off his thigh where I had had my body pressed next to his. He came back with a stack of towels, slipped them under my warm, sticky legs and butt, and flipped my pillow wet with tears. Then he slid in beside me, held me in his arms and rocked me gently. We didn't talk. Ray's parents called right then to tell us that Sloopy, our dog, had been full of cancerous tumors and died that morning. No mention was made of our crisis. We left for the hospital for a "D and C" that day; and years later, we named this baby Michael.

During the recovery period, I hung around the couch and bed, resting. I spotted, abstained from sex and found myself emotionally out-of-sorts. I talked to myself in the steamy bathroom mirror. My face pale and my eyes sunken, no makeup could help that face. I didn't fit into my regular clothes; and besides looking frumpy, I missed my mother, my sister, and my best friend, who were back in the States.

Here we lived upstairs in the last house on the left side of the main street in a little German town. The snow was wet and heavy, and between the large snowflakes, I could view the bright orange and parrot-green gas station next door. Sometimes for five or ten minutes, I counted the numbers of cars that pulled up to the pump, and sometimes I tracked the popular car colors of the hour. If I looked further on down the road, the two lanes wound through the Hunsruck Forest. I heard that wild boars roamed about, once even goring a forest meister to death. I had seen pictures of the large hogs and they were frightening animals—ugly. I was having an ugly day, and that's what this was about—just a damn-ugly day.

Later when the sun melted the snow, it slid slowly down the shingles on the little roof of the kitchen window right below us. I opened the large picture window and scooped handfuls of white from their small overhang—perfect for making Tori a snowman. Instead of going for an outing with Tori, we stayed inside to play. I stacked three different sized balls nicely on a turkey platter at the kitchen table. We used a carrot for a nose, marbles for the eyes and buttons. Tori poked a line of raisins for a mouth into the smallest snowball.

It was the brightest part of the day when I said, "Shall we give the snowman a bath?"

Tori nodded her head and followed me into the bathroom. We put him into the tub, and then when she aimed the hose and sprayed the water, Tori's eyes got bigger and her mouth opened wide until he was all gone.

She dropped the hose and cried, and I crouched down on the

floor and held her. "I'm sorry, I'm sorry."

What an ass I am. What was I thinking?

On the bottom of the big, German bathtub was one carrot, four marbles, seven raisins, a red ribbon and a tiny twig. She begged to save them, so I gave her an old jewelry box of mine.

The next day, I placed a big pile of baby clothes in a box to return to our generous friends and picked out a pink sleeper set for her dolly. Of course, Tori didn't understand why we were going to wait until later to have another baby. She was mad at God and me and refused to kneel down and say prayers anymore. That night I knelt down on the floor beside her bed and recited them aloud. She leaned against me with her eyes pinched closed and her mouth covered until I was finished. I wondered how a good mother would handle this. I stayed with her, sat on the floor beside her bed and watched her fall asleep. When her fingers relaxed, I slipped my hand out of hers and closed her door.

All of Our Problems and More

During the next year, alcohol became more of a problem.

First thing in the morning, I cleaned up, dumped any leftovers down the drain, added water to his bottles, and finally realized that I drank more than I wanted to in hopes that Ray would drink less—but he held unbelievable amounts of booze, until it became his own fragrance. I opened the door to the patio to freshen up the room.

For me, the first drink gave me a headache, another made it go away; and then, after three of anything, I was drunk, puked and wanted my mother. But I didn't want Mom to know anything about our marriage. I preached, begged him to stop, acted mad, then got extra nice and fixed his favorite food. Ray laughed at me. I was not myself. I gave in and wore no underwear around the house, and now . . . by now, I had missed two periods!

Ray held me close in his arms and put kisses all over my face.

"We get a fresh start," he said. "A new apartment came available on base housing, just down the street from the base nursery, and we get a new baby. This is terrific."

Ray softened his voice, stood with a slight sway to his hips, cupping his hands and somehow sexualizing his existence. *What was that?*

I stood feet planted securely on the floor facing him with thoughts bouncing all over in my mind.

How many months I would carry this baby? Don't tell Tori about it. No smoking, no drinking . . .

The next morning when we awakened, Ray asked me to do something I would never want to do. He asked me to write the intimate details of sexual encounters with all my old boyfriends.

"What?" I asked making a face.

"C'mon, please . . . Just do this for me," he said.

"No! I don't want to do that, much less think about it."

"You've got to. Please. Just do it for me."

I agreed so he'd stop pleading. Ray gave me a notebook and told me it was my homework. He left for work and said he'd catch coffee on base. I cried. Every hour I opened the blank page, stared at it for a few minutes responding with creepy feelings, and closed it. I chewed on my pencil and my stomach got sick. Ann Landers had said, "Never tell all." I didn't want to tell him anything. So, I copied small sections from a dirty book in his bedside drawer. Then I found another book in his closet and combined sexual scenes. It was believable to Ray who was so turned on he didn't know the difference. Then he wanted more stories, but I told him that was it, everything, and later that night he re-read my writings and made love to me.

Ray was not only a shameless eavesdropper in restaurants, but he commented on overweight people loud enough for them to hear. He made it a practice to sit with his back to the wall and face the door for safety. He smacked his lips at the sight of somebody gorgeous, made the *ummm* sound when he saw a beautiful leg or a voluptuous breast, even if they were within hearing distance; and my chest tightened, and my breath shortened. I was embarrassed and deeply disgusted with his behavior. I couldn't distract him from admiring his view; but when he photographed them, he'd whisper that I looked better than they did.

Something was wrong with us, and I didn't know how to fix it. I was frustrated when I had always been good at helping my friends find solutions.

It was at our house party. A few of the male guests made passes while I fixed food in the kitchen, flirted with suggestive words when I came from the bathroom, and became disgusting when I bent over to pick something dropped on the floor. Ray heard them, and Ray didn't say anything or step in. It aroused him, but by the time everyone left, I was pleased that he couldn't perform even if he wanted to.

Ray traveled TDY (temporary duty) frequently to *God knows where*. I rarely left the house, except maybe go down the street to the market in the village with the landlady. But Ray made sure someone single from his unit checked on us. I called them his spies, and when they dropped by, it was hard getting them to go home. They'd ask to stay over night if the weather was bad, and I wondered *what people would think*. I didn't sleep well with another man in my house.

Ray followed me around the house with his sophisticated camera, and I remembered that cheap Polaroid and the poodle. Now he developed his own pictures. Sometimes Ray flung the door open when I was dressing and flashed the damn thing and I'd yell at him. Other times he begged me to pose, but I felt dirty unless I'd been drinking and discovered unrecognizable parts of myself. His camera was the kind that had many parts, with a long, heavy lens he held with one hand, while he dialed numbers for close-ups with the other. Ray developed them on thick paper in black and white. Then he strung them across the bathroom on a clothesline. I saw cleavage and crotch shots that didn't look familiar; Ray told me to obey the "Do Not Disturb" sign hanging on the doorknob and to remember it was *only a hobby,* and he was married to me.

I didn't have a hobby. I had Ray.

When we bickered over money, I didn't know if Ray lied deliberately when I found unpaid bills in the gin box in the car, or if he just forgot. I picked little fights about that and his drinking. I wanted to go home because I missed my family, and I knew I wanted a divorce. But instead, when my sister came over for a visit, she thought our lifestyle was exciting and adventurous. During that month, she had a whirlwind romance with our friend, returned stateside and got married.

My parents told me I was not to come back for her wedding because it was too far and cost too much money. They'd send pictures. I was to stay put. I wanted to take Tori and leave, but I didn't know how to do that as a military dependent.

I told Ray that I was trapped and wanted out, and asked him what I should do. He said, *"Shut the fuck up!"* Not one of his friends would help me. In fact, I didn't know anyone who would stand up to Ray. The world was too darn big, and our bed was too small. I took my pillow into Tori's room and climbed under the covers on the top bunk. Ray followed, leaned his red face and minty booze breath against the mattress and apologized. I turned over to the wall. He closed the door laughing sarcastically and said, "Okay, but it's never gonna happen"

Tori slept while no one heard me scream except God.

Base Housing

I liked base housing, the idea of community and sharing the same language. The entire gray building was four stories high and held sixteen, two- and three-bedroom units. A huge back yard held swings and play equipment for all the families. We were on the second floor. The military jets flew over, and I had to read my neighbor's lips when we passed in the stairwell. Then she repeated herself, "Believe me, you'll get used to the noise and the rattling dishes."

The base movers set up our apartment within hours. One long, brown, tweed couch, wooden end tables, two over-stuffed chairs, a ginger jar lamp and a tall bar complete the living room. I placed a tall bouquet of mixed flowers and a copy of the latest *Better Homes and Garden* on the coffee table. Next to our bed was an empty crib, hopefully for a boy. I made up Tori's bunk and our double bed with fresh linens.

"You're nesting," my mother said on our brief call. It was a good word and my fresh start.

Ray was in the kitchen making sandwiches, but I was getting impatient to get the rooms just the way I wanted them. He measured everything, and I just looked and could tell where the nail belonged. I was like my mother that way. I climbed up on the step stool in Tori's bedroom to hang a ruffled valance. Losing my balance, I fell into her closet cushioned by empty cardboard boxes.

Ray came screaming from the kitchen, "Are you crazy? You can hurt yourself! You can hurt the baby." He scooped me up in his arms and my head fell on his shoulder. Briefly, it reminded me of the sweet "carried over the threshold" moment. Then he dropped me on our bed and yelled, "Stay there until I say you can move!" and slammed the door. It wasn't getting easier, but I thought I was getting better at it.

My English Friend

My next-door neighbor, Elizabeth, was a sweet English woman married to a black man with blue eyes. They had four children and we shared a balcony. Nearly every morning after the kids were off to school, I hurried over for English Breakfast tea with cream and sugar and rich, detailed conversations. Our daughters played together in the afternoon. I loved living here now because

I had a close friend and she even had an accent.

One morning the phone rang after Ray left for work. "Hi babe, I can see what you're wearing," a man said, breathing like he was having an asthma attack.

"You have the wrong number."

"No I don't."

"Who is this?" I asked, squatting on the floor.

"Some pervert," Elizabeth said at teatime. "I think there is one on every base."

The calls escalated for the next few days after Ray left for work. I stayed on the phone longer and he played soul music in the background. I planned to catch him myself somehow, but Elizabeth scared me. She said they know too much. He could follow me or come to the house when Ray was gone. So I stopped answering my phone and started my day off in Elizabeth's kitchen after our husbands and children were out of the house. She was like a big sister and checked on me frequently since this weirdo was brave enough to call at all hours, even when Ray was home. The caller hung up unless I answered. Ray grabbed the phone and told the son-of-a-bitch to leave us alone.

During the day, Ray and I had a signal where he rang once and hung up. Then I called back. The investigation of the phone stalker was short lived; the case closed but the calls continued.

"What do you mean the case is closed? Is this the military way to solve this problem—ignore it?" I said.

"Apparently it is. But don't question them. It's over, Emma."

"Tell me who it is. Do they know?"

"Yes, but he'll be gone stateside in two weeks so keep the blinds closed. He lives directly across the street and outranks me."

Soon . . . It Will Be Soon

Tuesday, September 28, 1971, after much pleading, I agreed to let Ray take a naked picture of me. Tori was asleep in her bunk; I undressed in front of the bar and draped my clothes over the back of the couch. My long hair covered my swollen breasts, but my fully stretched bulge grabbed his attention. I placed my warm hand on the side of my taut belly and a foot pushed gently and then somersaulted.

"Wait a second," I said, catching my breath, staring down at the lacquered parquet floor.

Ray lowered the camera. "Are you okay?" he asked, coming towards me.

"Yes." The loving look on his face made me think I was the most beautiful woman in the world, and he promised me he would never show this picture to anyone.

Then only an hour later, exhausted from the long day, I sat up in bed barely able to move with heartburn and puffy ankles. Ray propped the down pillows behind me and under my feet. I wanted to have my baby on my dad's birthday four days ago, but the doctor refused to induce me without a medical reason.

Early the next morning, I waddled down the hall to the bathroom. I held onto the towel bar and blew air out when my labor began. I had heard the second baby comes faster than the first, so I dressed quickly, put my hair in a ponytail and made sure Tori had her signed sheet for a kindergarten field trip and her Barbie lunch bucket. The house was in order. Elizabeth would watch for Tori after school.

When we got to the hospital, my contractions stopped, so I couldn't skip the grueling preparation. Instead, the nurse shaved me in places I could only view with a mirror, up my happy trail and to my belly button. Next, I paged through a Sears catalog and waited for the results of my enema. The nurse kept trying to hurry me up, but I wasn't finished. After sitting on the pot for one hour, I pried my red-ringed bottom off the toilet seat and climbed onto the gurney with help. I dilated to nine centimeters in the bathroom and acted quite smug, proud of myself, and gave directions, "Let's get this show on the road."

"We need a room, quick!" the nurse yelled.

℅

Right at lunchtime, three minutes past noon to be exact, I got my boy. Jimmy was 8 pounds 3 ounces and 21 inches—the largest and loudest baby in the nursery. He was an angel: a baby boy with a head of flaxen fuzz and big blue eyes. I loved him immediately.

My room soon filled with flowers. Roses from my parents and in-laws, carnations from my brother and sister, sun flowers from my friends and the most colorful mixed bouquet from the squadron. Each time a volunteer entered my room, I beamed, hoping it was a bouquet from the proud daddy, but Ray didn't send anything. I heard he was at the club celebrating and collecting bets. I wondered how I could be sad surrounded by a garden. I told myself it must be hormones.

I felt isolated in this double room with no roommate. The maternity ward didn't allow children, and dads had only designated short visits. I was in a restful sleep until a hot gooey bubble popped in my pants. I peeked under the covers and my pad was soaked through. I pulled my call light and waited. No one came. I needed relief from the pressure in my belly. I wanted to push or pee but didn't dare in my bed. I took my chances and headed for the bathroom with my IV pole. On the way, the room began to spin. *Take three giant steps* I told myself. I grabbed the string from the bathroom wall and pulled hard landing crooked on the toilet with the top of the IV pole tangled in the blinds over the window. When the nurse arrived, I was in a bloody mess and they whisked me back to bed. Right outside my room, the supervisor scolded the nurse assigned to me. And I was glad. After a bed bath, she massaged my fundus and did frequent pad checks through out the night. *She learned a valuable lesson, at my expense.* I needed her attention more than ever now.

The next day I wore my own nightgown, combed my hair and finished lunch. At four o'clock in the afternoon, there was a tapping sound outside my window. I pushed the food tray back and pulled up the shade. Tori pressed her sweet pigtails and face against the glass while her dad leaned on the building, grinning.

"Can I see my brother?"

I blew her a kiss and pointed to the little plastic crib, lifted Jimmy gently into my arms, turning him so she could get a good look and smiled at Tori's bright face, introducing them. I ignored Ray. He had been drinking—"*celebrating*" he said, since everybody in the bar was buying him a drink.

"Hi, Jimmy," she said expecting a response. Then she laughed, "He doesn't have any hair, but he's cute. Make his eyes open."

"Jimmy's sleeping right now. Later you can see his big blue eyes."

"I like him. Can you come home now? Can I help you with him?"

"I'll be home in a few days; and yes, Tori, you'll be a big help."

I heard a commotion in the hallway, said good-bye blew another kiss and pulled the shade. Ray yelled, "*We're going to the football game!*"

The door opened and the supervisor called out, "I heard voices in here. Do you have company in your room, Ma'am?" I closed my eyes quickly and as though I was asleep. She paused for a long moment, and then shut the door.

Two days later, Elizabeth welcomed us home with a pot of tea and hugs. We took pictures of Jimmy and opened the baby gifts from the States. I was still on a baby high. Ray was back at the shop.

The Military Inspections

I liked the military, probably because I loved our country. The security guards at the entrance waved the cars through the gate. Base housing rent came out of Ray's pay. We rationed gas, liquor and cigarettes like during wartime and got extra coupons from friends who didn't smoke or drink. It was easy to get around. Our chapel, grocery store, bookstore, hospital, gas station, nursery and clubs were located all in one area. I knew I was blessed. None of my friends had seen or been to the places I had been. Since Jimmy had dual citizenship, German and American, it meant he could choose which country he wished to serve when he turned eighteen years old.

Each year an annual squadron shop inspection happened, and no one took leave at that time. Today was the big day. I dried Ray's back, sat on the toilet seat and watched him shave. He pressed his uniform perfectly and his shoes reflected the split in his teeth. He told me his workbench was set up so no one could fault him. Ray looked spiffy this morning. He was proud of his accomplishments. I could tell he was nervous because he checked his armpits. I dared not hug him in case I wrinkled his shirt! He squeezed my hand and kissed Jimmy on the top of his head, and I whispered, "Good Luck."

Fifteen minutes later, I was in the kitchen having a bowl of cereal. Ray pounded on the front door so hard the little blue and white Dutch girl in the hallway fell off the wall and broke in two. He was screaming mad. "Help me find the scissor and a ruler— NOW dammit!"

I closed our bedroom door to muffle Ray's voice. The hair raised on my neck.

Ray banged on the medicine cabinet and kicked the tub. "I wouldn't re-up for those assholes, even if they begged me."

I fumbled through the junk drawer in the kitchen. "What happened?"

"Hold this," he said, handing me my magnifying mirror. "The

commanding officer, the son-of-a-bitch, measured my sideburns and sent me home to cut an eighth-of-an-inch off the left side."

"Are you kidding?"

"Fuck him! I'm telling you right now, we are out of here. I'm not staying in the military. I've had enough of their shit. I'm good at what I do! The length of my hair doesn't make a whole hell of a lot of difference."

"Hold the mirror still," he said, squeezing my hand too tight.

I used both hands so I didn't shake while Ray cut the tiny hairs and splashed cold water on his reddened face. He slammed the door and took off down the stairwell, two steps at a time. I hung up the towel and stared in the mirror at myself. I wondered about our future. Ninety days stateside was the projection—I could hardly wait.

Stop the Crying

Tonight I heard a baby cry, but it was not mine. It was the little boy in the upstairs apartment. He cried unevenly, choked, screamed and repeated the pattern until he was hoarse. The upstairs apartment, identical to ours, puts the parents above us and the baby above Tori's room.

"Are his parents deaf?" I asked sarcastically.

"Go to sleep," Ray said and turned over with his pillow, while Jimmy stirred in his crib.

"I wish he'd stop."

"Cover your head so you can't hear him."

"I still can . . ."

Three minutes pass. "Ray, dare me!"

"To do what?"

"Something . . . just say '*I dare you*' and I'll show you."

"Okay, I dare you . . . but don't go up there!"

My adrenaline surged. I saw this in a movie and always wanted to do it. I jumped onto the middle of our bed with the broom from the hall closet, grasped the straw whisks in both hands and beat on the ceiling with the handle. *Boom . . . boom, boom*! I caught my breath, regained my balance and doubled my booms. A loud thud overhead echoed with thumps down the hall, then voices and silence. I put the broom away and came back to bed. Ray snored softly on his side and I backed up against him like a bookend, matched my breathing with his and hugged myself before drifting off. The goodness inside of me was stirring. It was my first step toward child advocacy—something that wasn't popular and hadn't been named yet.

I avoided the upstairs neighbors in the stairwell the next morning. Elizabeth said they probably think Ray did it.

"Remember," I said, "they were the ones who gave Tori a more expensive doll than we did for her birthday party. Didn't her parents ever tell her it wasn't polite to outdo the parents?"

The Move

We celebrated Thanksgiving with friends, baptized Jimmy at six weeks of age and attended Midnight Mass in the base chapel for the last time. Today, January 18, 1972, I packed up holiday decorations and carefully wrapped my *Hummel* collection. The living room was bare. Eight German packers, men in coveralls, descended on our apartment carrying large shipping cartons, boxes, papers and tape. The word *"verboten"* was marked with masking tape in big black letters and strung across two cupboards to keep them from packing baby bottles, formula and the few items we needed for traveling.

I scrambled eggs and quickly finished breakfast. I turned to wash my pan and it was already wrapped in layers of long sheets of paper four times it's natural size and placed in a box. I removed the warm pan, unwrapped and washed it, wiped it out with a paper towel and handed it back. He didn't smile. He worked like a termite devouring everything in his sight. A full ashtray of butts got paper protection like a fine, glass figurine. We were able to ship three thousand pounds, but we had no furniture—mostly glass souvenirs and an orange, fake-leather footstool.

I ducked into another room and made a safe bed for Jimmy, who slept like an angel in a chest of drawers out of the way. I vacuumed last before we closed the door to our house and left to stay with friends until our flight. I was exhausted and clung to Elizabeth with a lingering embrace. She had been my angel and lifesaver, plus she made the best-ever English tea. I cried in the car.

"Are you hurt, Mommy?"

"No, I'm sad," I said and blew my nose. Tori patted my shoulder.

"It's okay," Ray said. "Hey, Liz promised to write."

A few miles down into a village, we came to a small wooden house that belonged to our friend, Bennie, and we gave him our car because he was a gentleman and a sweet person. When we came through his front door, I was ready to drop and was dying to take shower, but I canceled that plan. Clearly we had sauntered into a real party, and I couldn't take a shower because Bennie was there in his swim trunks with a bunch of women, who were partially clad in tee shirts; and he was spraying them with water. They stepped out onto towels, posed for photos, and showed off their hard nipples. The one who got the loudest cheers won. I covered Tori's eyes and headed toward the kitchen with Jimmy in my arms, hoping Tori didn't understand their anatomy or vocabulary. Ray said they were local pub girls.

"You're prettier than they are," he said leaning into me. "You'd win hands down."

"Right." I rolled my eyes as he joined the guys who were howling like wolves. Bennie gave us his bedroom right off the living room. Jimmy was safe and asleep in a top drawer, while Tori slept beside me. "Stop it, Ray."

"Oh come on. You know you like it."

I pushed his hand away from my breast and rolled him over

to the edge. The booze smell was strong. I bundled Tori in her own blanket and put her on the other side of me. Ray slid his hand between my legs and his fingers went limp as he fell asleep. I listened to them both breathing deeply and began to breathe their pattern until I slept.

Going Stateside

The new military 747 jumbo jet was full. It was a nine-hour flight out of Frankfurt, Germany to the States. Half way through our journey, a commotion in the front of the plane ended when a dentist delivered a baby in the aisle. It didn't take long before the baby boy and mother were doing well and the men smoked cigars with the father. We ate hot meals with glass dishes and silverware; snuggled with our kids under monogrammed blankets and small pillows, and thought good thoughts about our country, about our homecoming.

I changed Jimmy's diapers on the tray table and he ate, burped, pooped and slept across the Atlantic. As Tori played cards, colored, and completed a puzzle, all I could think about were my own parents. After all, it had been four years. Ray's clean-shaven face rested on the pillow and he read. When he drifted off to sleep, an eye opened each time one of us moved.

We entered the United States with exhilarating energy. The Statue of Liberty was visible from our window and the pilot said, "Please remain seated." Then he welcomed us home and played "The Star-Spangled Banner" over the intercom. We sang, yelled and clapped. Loud whistles rang out like the beginning of a sports event. When the music stopped, I still had my hand on my heart. We landed at Dover Air Force Base in Delaware. I air kissed the ground.

During our layover, I called my parents in North Dakota and said, "I'm home." But they said, "That's not your home." I told them *all* of this land was home to me now; it's the United States— *my* country I love.

ᔆᕀ

After Ray's discharge, we made our own decisions for the first time in our married life. We found a darling duplex not far from his parents. We told them the good news, and without even looking at the property, his mother said, "Find somewhere else! We don't like the landlord. He had bad dealings at our Realtor's office."

Ray said he never got along with his parents and it wasn't any better now. I was uncomfortable when his mother whispered to him. It was rude and they laughed like they had a secret again. But she did that when I first met her. She was the same but I had changed. It bothered me more now.

We sat at the kitchen table and talked after his parents had gone to bed. Ray said. "It's the day-late-and-dollar-short kind of thing telling me what to do. They weren't there when I needed them; I don't need them now."

I picked up the phone, dialed my parents, told them we were leaving in the morning and would see them for dinner. It was going to be the longest 363 miles ever. Even though my parents didn't like Ray, again they were polite. I hoped Ray would be different in civilian life. Everyone knew my family. It was a small town. People talked. My parents cried when I left the country, afraid something would happen to them while we were away. They stayed healthy and now my father talked for three minutes and hung up, but Mom, well she stayed on the line and caught up with me.

I had never seen my dad hold a baby. He lifted Jimmy up into the air, his little butt in the palm of his hand, and said, "Hello buddy." Jimmy's eyes widened and his little mouth grew to an amazing toothless smile. I snapped a picture. We cheered and Jimmy cried. Dad handed him back to me and left the room with Tori.

"It wasn't you, Grandpa," Tori said. "It scares baby Jimmy when we clap."

Then Mom, in her best magenta sweater and tweed pants, held Jimmy. Proudly, I said, "This is your grandma," but Mom corrected me. "Don't call me grandma! I'm not that old and I'm not doing any babysitting." I stood corrected. Mom had passed down another generation of first-name grandparents and no built-in babysitters.

Tori called her grandma "Morning." Tori heard "Good morning" so many times, she one day blurted out, "Hi Morning!" and it stuck. This name thrilled my mother. The incident of naming is similar for Jimmy. After each bite of baby food spooned into Jimmy's mouth, Mom said, "thank you or *taaataaaa.*" Then one day Jimmy clenched his lips together, gave mother a penetrating stare and yelled, "Hi *Tata!*" My delighted mother kissed his chunky cheeks. "Hello everybody. I have another new name—I'm Jimmy's *Tata.*" The name stayed with her until her death at 91.

~~~~

Within a week we found a two-bedroom apartment, six blocks from Mom and Dad. Ray got a job as a television technician and moonlighted as a bartender at the Elks Club. I was alone most evenings and talked frequently on the phone with my mother. Ray's folks gave us their eight-foot green couch and a chair and bought themselves a new set. We made bookcases from bricks and stained boards, and put our small television on the top shelf. My *Hummel* collection was in my antique teacart from Holland, near the front door. Tori slept in a big old wrought iron bed, and Jimmy shared her room with his crib. Our bedroom doubled as an office, but someday I was going to have a bedroom that was only a bedroom.

One night Ray and I left for the movies while the landlord's daughter babysat for us. When I came through the front door, I smelled glue and saw newspapers spread over the kitchen table.

"Those are my *Hummels!*" I shrieked.

"I know. I'm gluing the head back on this one. And you can hardly tell the top of the broom broke off here," she said. "But this goose is a mess. I can probably fix it."

I'm still shrieking. I didn't know my voice could go so high.

"Who did this?!"

"Oh, Jimmy was tiptoeing around the coffee table, and when he lost his balance, he plopped down on the floor and grabbed the tea cart door on his way down. They all tipped over. He broke thirteen of them."

"Omigod." Ray put his hand on my shoulder.

"I can't begin to afford to replace these. Tell your parents what's happened here tonight or I will. How could you let this happen?" Ray turned me around and nudged me out of the room.

He fished in his pocket for her pay and opened the door for her to leave. The babysitter didn't answer or look at us. I cried. Some of the figurines I purchased from the Berta *Hummel* Factory at Roedental, Germany. They were my only items of value.

I was so upset I wanted to be alone. I watched Johnny Carson while Ray wandered to bed. I counted thirty-six advertisements during the show. I tried to tell myself it didn't matter, that they are just ceramic pieces, but I was unconvincing. It wasn't Jimmy's fault, but I already knew I'd tell him about this when he was older. I remembered stuff like this. I wish I didn't, but he was forgiven—the babysitter wasn't.

House Hunting

Because we both thought renting was like throwing money out the window, I house hunted while Ray worked. Our Realtor told me about an unlisted home, move-in ready, located in my old neighborhood. I had never been inside this one, but I already knew I wanted to live there. It had lots of possibilities. Two stories—white with black shutters, a fenced back yard carpeted with red and yellow leaves, peonies, more trees, and a garage. I jumped with excitement when my father approved of our selection. Our house payment was $179 per month. It was only three doors from my favorite aunt and two blocks up the street from where I was raised.

Ray suggested I find a job at the hospital to make this purchase easier, and I agreed to interview. It was scary since I didn't have any idea where I would fit in.

"A graduate nurse? We have no such listings."

I pushed my pride aside, explained the situation, accepted the position of desk clerk, completed my paperwork and thanked her. Placed on payroll, I started immediately on the third floor of Mercy Hospital.

While I was at the clinic for a work physical, my family doctor thought I was an RN. I told him I hadn't passed my boards, had two kids, moved overseas, et cetera. My excuses sounded lame, even though they were true. The heat of shame rose up from my breasts to my neck and I fussed with the buttons on my blouse.

"Listen here," he commanded. "I expect you to *take* your boards and *pass* your boards. You can do it. I'm counting on you."

"But . . . but doctor," I stammered, "I don't know where to begin."

"What? I don't believe you. Call the State Board. Talk to them. Get on the stick."

"It's not that easy . . ." I said.

Two seconds later, in a booming voice, he *dared me* to take my boards and then bet that I *couldn't* do it. I had a sudden fight response in my gut when he challenged me. I was determined. I would do this! Some day I'd wear RN on my nametag. He shook my hand to seal the deal and abruptly left the room.

The Next Move

Over the next few weeks, I called the State Board of Nursing and begged them to consider me as a Candidate. They told me that I had to prove that I was a serious contender and explain to the board exactly how I would prepare for my testing, since I was no longer in school. I figured a study course for myself over the next year, put it in writing and sent it off in the mail. I received an acceptance letter and was given a date to test the following year. I worked full-time on the three-to-eleven shift, questioned every doctor's order, and on my days off, sat in an empty room at the junior college at noon watching movies to review the basics. I brushed up on medications and read nursing journals and case studies. At first I didn't tell anyone my plans for fear of failure; but by now everyone knew what I was doing, and my co-workers supported me.

The afternoon before my examination, we drove four hundred miles and stayed in a motel across the street from the testing site. The kids set out for the pool with their dad. I dug in my purse for the last two green and white capsules from an old, stressed-out gut problem after Germany—I wanted a good night's sleep. No one needed to know how scared I was. I swallowed one while the other was stashed in my pocket for morning. I didn't want my stomach to betray me.

I was unable to finish my eggs and hash browns that morning. Ray took my slice of toast and put it on his plate. I kissed Ray good-bye and he whispered, "Good luck. You can do it."

I crossed the street at the light, begging God for a retentive memory. The overcast sky was like a reminder that this was my last chance. I beat the Serenity Prayer out of my feet saying a word with each step:

"God... grant... me... the... siren-it-ty... to... ac-cept" until my confidence returned. I worked up the spit in my mouth, put the capsule on my tongue and swallowed. Then I proceeded to the alphabetically marked doors of the auditorium.

Two hundred chattering women, all strangers to me, stood in front of closed doors. Pockets of young girls, classmates I'd guess, hung back on the sidewalk questioning one another. The voices got louder the longer we waited. I put my cardigan sweater on and tried not to listen. Then electronic doors swung wide open. It was hushed now except for the sandpaper sound of nylon stockings rubbing together and footsteps. We proceeded to our assigned sections. Each person sat several feet apart at long tables and listened to the intercom spew out the instructions. Monitors passed out papers, the timer began and we were under their watchful eyes. This part was familiar.

I put down the first answer that came to mind and moved on, dulling both of my number two pencils. Every few minutes a page turned and someone cleared their throat or sneezed. If I didn't know the answer, I skipped it and returned. And when I finished, I ascended hundreds of steps to the doorways, looked back, dropped my test papers into a slot, my pencils into a box and headed out into the glaring sun and sighed.

Ray was in the front of the building leaning against a pillar, smoking a cigarette. I walked rapidly straight into his body. He stood up straighter and tried to read me. I had no idea about the results. I smiled only because it was over, not because I thought I had passed. He lit up another cigarette and placed it to my lips and we headed back across the street for the kids and a drink.

Even though I knew it would be at least six weeks before I heard how I did, I checked the mail each day. I played silly mind games like *okay, I won't check and maybe it will come.* And it happened that way. Ray called me during my three-to-eleven shift at the hospital.

"It's here," he said.

"Omigod, are you holding it?"

"Yes. Do you want me to open it?"

"No. No, no . . . don't you dare. It's mine."

"I'm holding it up to the light. It's thin and folded. I wonder what that means."

"Ray, don't open my mail. I mean it. I'll be home at 11:15."

I pulled up in the dark driveway and the front yard burst into light. Rockets shot straight up into the clear sky. Tori and Jimmy had sparklers, made wide circles, and yelled, "Mom passed! Mom passed!"

Ray pulled me out of the car and twirled me around. I hooted and hollered while the neighbors flicked their yard lights off and on.

"Thank you God!" I screamed. Now I would always have a job. I could take care of the kids and myself if anything ever happened to Ray.

The mattress dipped in the middle for the weight of his heavy body and I rolled into him. He slept soundly but I couldn't keep my eyes closed. I stared at the ceiling happy, except for one thing. It bothered me that Ray opened my mail after I asked him not to peek. He did whatever he wanted even if it wasn't legal. I shuddered—*what if I had not passed*.

A large sheet cake in the break room covered the table below a pink poster with everyone's name and congratulatory well-wishes. Propped up on the phone at my nurses' station, a small sealed envelope held a card that said, "*Congratulations, glad I lost our bet. Sincerely, Doctor K*".

I floated, not literally, to all the wings and loved each one of them. I was a dedicated nurse, wore support hose, a starched uniform and a nursing cap with one velvet stripe. I washed my hands *before and after* I went to the bathroom, ate popcorn from a bedpan, substituted a tongue blade for a spoon and charted using pens printed with names of prescription drugs.

Ray's Shop

I switched to the eleven-to-seven graveyard shift, temporarily, at the hospital to make more money. Ray rented a building and started dealing in antique collectibles, jewelry and coins. I selected the navy floral wallpaper for the shop and Ray hung it. The deep shades of blue highlighted the antique cabinets' curved glass shelves. I washed the glass, polished the silver and vacuumed the floors. Ray said our plan was a good one. The kids had their homework done and were in bed when I left for work at night.

Ray habitually spent half the night up working at home

cataloging and grading materials anyway. He seemed to function on little sleep. And I never missed out on dinner time with the family, school functions or meetings. I crawled in and snuggled with him before he left for work. Sometimes he took the kids to school and came back home, but I swallowed my yawns at functions and carried on life with less than the recommended amount of desired sleep. If I had only known that someday I would come to regret this decision to work a night shift.

At first I was proud to be involved in the background at the shop and happy for Ray, but then over the months, I lost more trust when I overheard a conversation at the store between Ray and a customer who was an older woman from our community. He habitually embellished stories about the history behind previous ownership of gems and/or how he came about getting them—lies told in a most persuasive manner. When the woman left, I stared at him.

"Do you know who that was you were telling all that stuff to?"

"It doesn't really matter. She'll be back." Ray rubbed up next to me and picked up a diamond tennis bracelet. "If you can't dazzle them with brilliance," he said rotating the gems back and forth to catch the light, "baffle them with bullshit!"

"Sign this," he said.

"Sign what?"

"Put your John Henry on our quarterly tax report and don't ask so many questions—*geez.*"

In the back of my mind, a neon sign flashed, *"Don't sign anything."* I hesitated for a second too long and he grimaced, "What the hell's the matter; don't you trust me?" I didn't answer; it was easier to sign than argue, even though I knew I'd somehow regret it.

I didn't want Tori to go to the shop after school, but Ray declared emphatically that he needed her to help him. At home, Tori practiced the piano for hours instead of picking up her room, so I closed her door. Jimmy wanted his bed made every morning and tossed his junk in his closet. The weekends ended up in a cleaning frenzy. I added pressure by inviting my parents over. My father was the fire inspector. Ray thought he examined our house like a snoop and locked the door to his private office.

It was my day off and I made Mrs. A.J.'s hot dish with hamburger and potatoes and carrots. Tori set the table, Jimmy put his dinosaurs away and the three of us prayed and ate. Ray wasn't home. I was so tempted to call the bar again, but I had done that before; and it only made things worse when he said he'd be right home and didn't come. The kids finished dinner and were off in the other room when the door slammed hard. There stood Ray.

Wired Shut

"Omigod, what's happened to you?"

His swollen face distorted his eye and he was drunk. He choked, spit blood on the floor and wiped his bloody nose on his shirtsleeve, handing me a soaked bar towel. He tried to talk. I couldn't understand him and that made him angry. His breath was ragged and he was clearly hurt. I pushed him back out the door to my car because I didn't want the kids to see their father.

"Tori, take care of your brother. I'll be back in a bit."

"What's the matter, Mom?"

"Nothing! Do as I tell you."

"Two assholes jumped me in the bathroom. I (cough) did *not* do (cough) anything wrong!"

"Shut up, Ray. Hold the rag over your mouth."

We sped up the street straight to the hospital. I was so pissed off, not so much about the injury as his shameful drunkenness; and now my colleagues will know that he's far from the perfect husband that I had portrayed. Worse yet, I was glad someone shut his arrogant embarrassing mouth.

I drove into the familiar ambulance entrance as if it was

my own garage and tooted my horn. We didn't have to wait; my supervisor immediately helped us out. Ray refused to sit in a wheelchair and staggered into the back door on her arm. She paged the doctor and cleaned him up, while I stepped outside the curtain and did the paperwork. I didn't want him to talk to me or glance my way because I was upset enough to cry. The staff didn't look at me either; but with utmost respect, they all worked on Ray. After the x-rays, Doc called in a specialist who arrived in minutes and scheduled surgery for a fractured jaw.

Dr. Chin, the surgeon, pulled me aside in ER and shoved the x-ray up on the lighted box. He affirmed Ray's story that this type of fracture can only come from behind and with great force. Then he demonstrated the blow. At that moment, I was humiliated. I hadn't believed Ray. He was telling the truth and then got his mouth wired shut. I smiled back at Dr. Chin, who *did* help make this story easier to tell. For once Ray was the victim.

After discharge from the hospital, I placed the wire cutters at the head of the bed in case of an emergency. If needed, I was the one responsible to cut the wires so he wouldn't choke to death. I told him he had better treat me nice or I might lose the cutters.

"*Arrrrh*" sounds came through his gritted teeth, but he was at my mercy.

This was my "*when something bad happens, good can come from it.*"

Ray sipped all his meals through a straw. He rode a bicycle, no longer shaved, and had a premature graying beard and a brown mustache that hid his scar. Ray dropped fifty pounds—looked like he did when I married him. Even though Ray sipped malt beer in tall cans through the straw, his jaw healed in a few months, the wires were removed, and waa-laaaaaah, he was back again for round two or three, or four—I didn't know anymore.

The Call for Help

Calls came from collections, and Ray got mad and complained about my complaining. Everything was my fault these days, but I didn't understand why at the time. I would rebut what he said and defend myself, which gave Ray his free pass to leave the house, and of course, head for the bar. It worked for him every time. He snagged me before I knew it. And sometimes, with my truth being told, I did it on purpose.

After the kids were asleep, I rocked back and forth in the chair and had another *heady* conversation with Ray who *wasn't* home. No one was around. I smoked my last cigarette, argued with myself and then looked up Al-Anon in the phone book. I needed help.

"This is the Al-Anon help line. My name is Karen; how can I help you?"

I waited, thinking it was a recording and recognized the voice of my co-worker from the hospital. I grabbed a Kleenex, covered the mouthpiece and disguised my voice.

"I don't mean to be rude, but if my husband comes home, I'm hanging up. I don't want him to catch me."

"That's okay. I'll give you our meeting place and time, in case that happens."

"I don't know what to do anymore," I told her. "I use a code on the calendar and keep track of the days he drinks. And now, it's every day." She listened to me tell stories about his drunkenness and then assured me I wasn't crazy—I didn't cause it, and I couldn't cure it.

The back door opened. "Okay Mom; thanks for calling!"

"No, I didn't buy you any cigarettes," he slurred and tossed a flat pack containing only one smoke.

"Thanks. Good night."

He headed downstairs to his office and I went to bed.

I hung onto the crumbs of comfort from Karen for a long time but then convinced myself again I could handle his drinking, each day hoping it would stop. It was one year later when I reached my bottom and attended my first Al-Anon meeting: September 23, 1984.

I remember that morning . . .

I changed the living room around in inches, moved the chair a little to the left, switched a picture and tilted a mirror. Then I stood on a step stool and unhooked the drapes—all of them. I could see two blocks down the street. It was like a fishbowl now and I liked it. I could breathe easier.

"You're crazy. Do ya hear me woman? Damn crazy," Ray said.

"You're right, Ray. You think you're always right, and this time you are."

"You need help," he said, mashing his cigarette butt out in his saucer.

"I know. I'm getting help tonight."

"And how do you plan to do that?"

"I'm going to an Al-Anon meeting. And do you know why, Ray?"

"You're crazy!" he yelled and slammed the door on his way out.

"You drink too much!" I screamed back.

I opened my trembling hand, unfolded the sweaty wrinkled piece of paper: *"7:00 p.m., Broadway and Main—up narrow stairwell, first room on the right, past bathroom."* I put it in my pocket.

~~~~

Tonight before I left for work at the hospital, I dozed off on the couch while the family watched television. Ray, without warning, attacked the wall with a buzz saw to expand the room. I woke up—the wall was gone. The air was smoky and it was dead quiet except for their laughter. That was when I realized my level of exhaustion from working nights. I was still shaking when I arrived at the hospital, but we eventually completed the basement in stages: painted the cement walls red; added a loud, multi-colored carpet; purchased an art and drawing table for Jimmy, and doctored up the bar so it was usable.

My parents came to see our newly-finished basement family room. We played a game of bumper pool and had a picnic dinner of baked ham, beans, potato salad, a green salad and dessert. Dad won. I told Mom she didn't have to help me carry all the mess back upstairs, but she insisted. She dropped a glass jar of Russian dressing on the floor, and it ran like blood across the pattern. Even though I said it was okay and not to worry, it wasn't because the stain was permanent. It then became a focal point in this confetti-patterned rug. Ray said to ignore it.

Some days I hated myself. Why did I pick that carpet? It looked like a fruit bowl puked and now I hated it.

Jimmy's Accident

I finished the dishes, poured cold water through my Mr. Coffee for tea and got Tori into the bathtub. As usual, I asked her to sing so I would know she was okay while I was out in the kitchen. Ray was reading in the living room, and Jimmy ran through the house with his airplane extended over his head, making engine noises. I folded the damp towel, hung it up, wrung out the dishrag, and got ready for a quiet evening. The phone rang. Mom called to apologize again for ruining the carpet.

Tori yelled for a washcloth from the bathroom, and Jimmy barreled into the kitchen, straight to the unattached towel cabinet to get her one. When he pulled both doors open, it tipped away from the wall, and my Mr. Coffee pot, filled with hot water, slid toward Jimmy.

"Jimmy!" I screamed and threw the receiver on the table.

He turned to me when he heard his name and saved his face but scalded his delicate creamy neck, right arm and chest. His screams pierced through the house. His skin turned bright pink, and he fell to the floor kicking and thrashing. Ray leaped from the living room to Jimmy's side and took him into his arms. I dumped water on him from the faucet, soaked a white sheet and wrapped him in it, all in a matter of seconds. I grabbed the phone off the floor and dialed Mercy ER.

"Stop a doctor! My son's burned. It's bad—we're on our way!"

With this commotion, my mother and dad came for Tori immediately when we left.

Two doctors and two nurses were waiting when we pulled up into the ambulance entrance in our red Ford Pinto.

"Help us!" I screamed through the opened windows.

They rushed to him, removed the sheet and cut off his clothes. I stood nearby and out of the way. Jimmy stared at me with a look of terror in his darkened eyes. They started an IV and gave him something to ease the pain, while I held his hand. After the debridement, they wrapped Jimmy in fluffy gauze and admitted him to Pediatrics.

I headed home to dress for work. The house was dark and empty. Water still trickled from the faucet. I kicked the counter. I screamed, wailed and made a sound I'd never heard before. I lay on the orange shag carpet in the living room on my stomach and pounded my fists into the floor. No words came out of me, only louder screams, gulping sobs, begging God to heal Jimmy and make the pain in my gut go away. I vomited and showered.

Ray stayed with Jimmy from seven in the morning to three in the afternoon; I sat with him from three to eleven at night. Then I worked the eleven-to-seven shift. This lasted ten solid days, around-the-clock. Ray and I passed each other. He got out of bed and I crawled in and put my body into the warm spot that held his. His smell lingered and I breathed deeply to suck it all up, until there was no more. He tucked me in. He kissed me gently. I heard the door close, the car started and I dropped off instantly from exhaustion. Ray took Tori to school, hung the closed sign in the shop window and headed for the hospital.

In the afternoon I accompanied Jimmy to physical therapy.

I liked all the therapists, and because of that, I guess I expected they would be nice to Jimmy, who loved the water. But when his dressings came off and the forced water whirled about his raw chest and arm, he screamed and stiffened. His eyes rolled back in his head and they held him like they were filleting a fish. Bits of skin floated in the water.

"Stop!" I screamed.

"Leave . . . now," said the therapist without looking away from Jimmy.

I didn't want to, but I knew I had to because I couldn't stand to watch them torture my baby.

"This is absolutely necessary," he continued. "Now go. Wait in his room for us."

Desperate, I headed for the chapel, prayed, and cried. It seemed like I was always asking God for strength and courage. Was I supposed to figure out how to get through all this painful stuff on my own? The horrific, daily cleansing procedure eventually left his rice paper skin spotless, without any evidence of trauma and soft like a baby. And while they worked on him, I knelt in the chapel and found peace. It lasted only for that day, until next time, and then I came back to prayer. That pattern held true from one crisis to another through out my life.

Valentine's Day was extra special because Jimmy was coming home. In anticipation of his arrival, I scrubbed his room down with strong solutions, stacked dressings and jars of Silvadene cream in the hall closet, blew up balloons and bought a heart-shaped ice cream cake from the Dairy Queen. I was his full-time mother and nurse for the rest of the week. I watched him like a bug under a glass while he chewed his gum until all the sugar was gone.

Now I knew what our families in Pediatrics experienced. I would be a better nurse. I would be a better mother. But I had to talk to Tori because she was being too quiet. I never seemed to get enough time with her. She played piano for the school choir and practiced for hours in the living room—plus she had band practice. What a gifted girl.

Life on Ewing Street

I scrambled the eggs, added whole milk, tilted the bowl, and *knew*. Even without knowing, I knew something was wrong with us again. Ray worked all the time. There wasn't even 'make-up sex' anymore. He had the headache or was too tired. Since I smoked and was at risk for an embolus on birth control pills, Ray insisted on getting a vasectomy. I signed the papers. But I didn't know that it wasn't me he was worried about getting pregnant.

I didn't enjoy the company of old friends because none came around. We were all too busy trying to get ahead of one another. Ray didn't like any of the men married to my friends. He hung out with young guys from work and provided alcohol; and I'd call him a bad influence on them. *His buddies,* he said. At parties, they always talked about their last drunk, but they didn't call it *getting drunk*—it was about the *fun* they had. Of course, Ray stayed composed around them. He drank anyone under the table and never bottomed out.

My best friend lived thirteen blocks from my house. We saw each other once a year at the drugstore, usually during the holidays. It was, *"Hello, how are you" "We must get together sometime,"* and *". . . you look great,"* then we hugged and said good-bye. We never asked about husbands, and there was no time to talk about children. I was lonely.

You should have seen me act out (although back then I didn't know that language). I mowed the lawn in a fury. The blades knocked chips off the pinecones and little rocks struck at my mud-splotched shoes. It was loud, but the noise helped break my ugly suspicious thoughts. I mowed like I vacuumed—back and forth and sideways, seven times in the same spot, until only smooth dirt remained under the trees.

One day the lawn mower belched smoke, chugged and sputtered. My arm felt ten feet long after repeated yanking on the pull cord. Thin, cold, sweat oozed down in front of my ears and dripped on my sleeveless blouse; and grass clippings stuck to my bare legs. Judge Paulson, my neighbor from across the street, came over and offered a hand. He was a lifesaver. The ironic thing, is that my good neighbor, the judge, saw me a week later in his courtroom for a speeding violation. When I explained that Ray forgot to tell me the speedometer reading was inaccurate, he told me to make *him* pay the fine. Then he banged his gavel and asked for the next case. I called him an asshole in my head, but I happened to like that judge.

What Eats Away at Me

The next few years were stagnant; our life ran by like weather with more than four distinct seasons. The readings were simply hot, very hot, mosquitoes, sun burns, cold, very cold, frostbites, chapped lips and luckily a few weeks of perfect warm and cool. Each step got faster in our routine. I washed clothes, mowed the lawn, shoveled the sidewalk; we ate one meal a day together at home; I cleaned the house on the weekends and attended every performance that involved our children.

I never thought of Ray while I was at work. He left town at least once a month, and I missed him and waited by the phone when I got home. We checked on each other. He drank too much and partied too often, which worried me. But when he held me, kissed me and said everything was fine, I believed him—because I had to believe him. But I lied to me. I wrote poetry about being lonely and read it to my aunt, who thought it was quite interesting, since I was married. She said keep writing, but don't dwell on misery because we looked good; but I already knew *that* didn't mean anything.

Without warning, I woke up with a deep stomach pain below my belly button that scraped my innards. I took short sips of air and became more lightheaded and weak. The house was quiet and overly warm. I hung onto the railing and carefully placed one foot at a time on each stair. Something was terribly wrong.

"Where is everybody?" I called out. "Anyone home?" Ray bounded around the corner and broke my fall when I collapsed.

"Admit for observation" was on the script in my hand. I had to ride in a wheelchair to the medical wing from the doctor's office. The tests were inconclusive and the pain faded after the shot. I wasn't pregnant. Ray had his surgery, but instead of the anticipated increase in activity, our sex life was slim.

"Rest," the doctor said. "You're working too hard."

I knew he was right, with school and a new job. The kids and I did our homework together at the kitchen table. I put untiring effort into getting my degree in nursing at the University of Mary—I'd prove to Ray I wasn't stupid.

Ray paced about my room. Then he took my hands and, casting his eyes downward, smiled. "I want you home from the hospital. Besides, I'll take good care of you. We leave in the morning for the Knights of Columbus Convention."

"You still want me to go? After this fiasco?" I asked. "I'm still on a liquid diet."

"You can stay in the hotel room—get room service. I want you with me and the kids. You know how much they are looking forward to this trip."

And after more begging, kisses and hugs, that was exactly what happened. Ray was the boss. Instead of recovering in bed at home, I pleased him against my own will. We drove 132 miles north and checked into our poolside room at the hotel. The kids hit the pool; I begrudgingly attended the Ladies Luncheon, while Ray accessed the Hospitality Suite. I downed three flavors of gelatin salads, leaving the lettuce on my plate, and drank several glasses of plain 7UP on ice, with a twist of lemon. I relished a fancy hotel room—the fresh sheets, the French soaps and the privacy.

I waited for Ray, and I waited some more, and then undressed. The kids slept, but I was vigilant. It was midnight. My romantic fixation dissipated. I was alone, unable to sleep and pissed. I set the alarm for 7:00 a.m. so Ray could get up and shower for the tomorrow's events, but when it buzzed off in the morning, he had not returned to the room.

"How are *we* feeling?" he asked.

It was a few minutes after seven, and Ray sat on the edge of the bed with his hand on my forehead. His warm breath tinged with booze and smoke, a film of sweat on his unshaven face and his stale cologne was nauseating. I reared up from the bed and pulled the damp twisted sheets around my shoulders.

"There's no *we* here; and besides, what the hell do you care? You didn't even come home last night."

"Home?"

"Don't make light of this. You know what I mean."

With smug confidence he said, "Good morning to you, too. Look, I'll make it up to you. I promise," and walked over to Jimmy who welcomed him warmly. He winked at Tori and made a funny clicking sound with his mouth. They got back into their suits and headed for the pool. He gave them money for video games, and I watched the kids through the glass window and ordered breakfast. Ray showered after a twenty-minute nap and was ready to leave. I never understood how he could go with so little sleep.

~~~~

We stopped at a Chinese restaurant on our way out of town. We didn't have one in our hometown, so this was a treat; but then, so was McDonald's. But Jimmy was out-voted this time and we didn't see Ronald. We were the only patrons seated in a bright red vinyl booth; a lantern hung down over our heads. Chopsticks were lined up beside our silverware. It was cold, and the Chinese music didn't warm things up.

Tori ate whatever her dad told her to have. I was never sure what I wanted, and Jimmy said, "I'll have a Chinese hamburger."

"It not on menu, but I make for you," she said with a slight bow of the head.

His wreath of smiles made me giggle. How sweet and funny he was. No one talked. I had tea. Ray had a scotch and soda. Next, the waiter brought us white puffy appetizers.

"Why we are eating egg cartons?" Jimmy asked, and I finally

laughed for the first time. It broke the silence.

"Good observation, Jimmy. Want one?"

"No thanks."

"*No thank you* is the proper way to say it. Now try one," Ray said.

"But I don't want to."

"Well, I want you to."

"Ray, Jimmy doesn't want to,"

"Okay, have it your way. There's more for me to eat then." He glared with an arched eyebrow at Jimmy, who dropped his chin.

The ride home on the narrow road was quiet. For a few miles we read aloud the gigantic billboards and sipped sodas. After twenty minutes, the kids fell asleep. While the soft music played on the radio, Ray slid his hand over to my thigh and rubbed back and forth, watching the road and smiling. I looked straight ahead and closed my eyes. He always fed my skin hunger.

The Birds and the Bees

My mother thought I'd do the best job of explaining the facts of life to my sister, who was seven years younger than I was, only because I was attending nursing school. When I sat on the bed with her, she giggled and said her friend had already told her.

Now that I had my own daughter, it was different. I wanted to say just the right things to protect her for the rest of her life. I quoted something from an old pamphlet that I loved, with a picture of the Blessed Mother on the cover. I began, *"Don't let a fool kiss you and don't let a kiss fool you."* I said it twice to emphasize the importance. She nodded and waited for more. I talked about French kissing and breasts. She folded her hands, unfolded them, twisted the bow on her dress, and looked me right in the face. She didn't giggle or blush. She listened. I told her not to let *anyone* touch her private parts down there. And we hugged and it was over.

It was after our talk when a naked man, wearing only a brown raincoat, jumped out from behind the old school bus and flashed Tori, who was in middle school. She was upset and scared and told her dad, who told me. The school officials related to us that seven girls reported being molested after watching a television program over the Christmas holidays. Apparently, Rebecca on "Days of Our Lives," molested in one of her scenes, said to *tell someone.*

Tori called me into her room.

"Mom, look at this spot on my arm."

"What about it?"

"It feels funny and it looks weird."

I ran my index finger along the soft short hairs on her arm. "Tori, it's only a freckle," and I bent to kiss it. "Is that all?"

"I guess," she said rubbing the spot until it was red.

The next day it happened again, "Mom, look at my leg—here by my knee. It's a bump."

"Did you bump into your bed?"

"I don't know, Mom."

"It's a little bruise. You've run into something," and I kissed that too. "C'mon; let's set the table for supper." I had no idea that what she was showing me or wanted me to see, wasn't visible to the naked eye.

~~~~

I noticed how we sat in Mass, and even walked around as a family, unlike other families. I complained to Ray because Tori was on his far right, Jimmy was on his left and I was on the end. When we traipsed through the parking lot, Ray walked ahead holding Tori's hand and Jimmy and I pulled up the rear. Something didn't feel right, but Ray laughed with a big open mouth and licked his mustache. He made direct eye contact, pressed the stiff hairs down on his chin as if he was petting something, and said I had a crazy imagination.

Fixing Up the Place

I folded our dried clothes on a vintage Formica table, a red cracked-ice pattern with hairpin chrome legs in our make-shift utility room that shared the same space as the small freezer and large furnace. Ray hung shelves for me in front of the crawl space with books on one side and laundry supplies and poisons, like bleach and peroxide, on the other. I secretly started saving money for any kind of emergency and needed a place to hide it, so I stood on the step stool and reached as far back as possible into the crawl space. I touched something with my fingertips, a funny shaped thing—a tube, with a bowl on the end, like an old pipe. Ray would know where it came from.

"What do you mean, it's a *bong*? You mean like . . . '*Cheech and Chong*' bong?"

"It's a bong. I've answered your question. Now give it to me."

"No. You can't have it. I don't want anyone using this in my house."

"Well, it's not mine." Ray laughed. "It belongs to a friend of mine."

"What friend?"

"I'm not telling. Obviously, you'll have no respect for him if you know."

"I'll suspect everyone you have over, Ray."

"Well, at least I have friends over."

"That's not fair. I work all the time."

"I work *and* I have friends," he said."

I palmed it, and like a defiant child said, "Finder's keepers," and put my hand behind my back.

"Go ahead smarty, but you don't know what you're doing. You could get me in trouble."

When Ray walked away, I threw it overhand as hard as I could into the crawl space.

Monday Was Washday

I swore Tori needed a trap door on her floor for a closet. I was never quite sure which stack was clean and which one needed washing. I sniffed, checked pockets and guessed. I had plenty of washed-out dollar bills, but this time it was a note. Something told me not to read it, but I was her mother and it was okay to look. Before I left the room, I unfolded it and read the words written by Ray. There was no date on it but it said *"Sweetheart,"* and talked about yearning. Of course, it was Ray's writing—the slight slant to the left and the slashes made on his *t's.*

Tori shouldn't have read this note; and how did she get it? Behind her bedroom door, a white cotton dress with store tags hung on a padded hanger—lacy, sexy, in an innocent kind of way with a see through bodice, short sleeves and full skirt. I hadn't seen that before either. *What's up with the dress?* I held it up in front of me, but it was excessively small. I hung Tori's robe back over the dress exactly how I found it and tossed the note.

Jimmy, Tori and I were hungry. Browned pork chops in mushroom gravy with mashed potatoes and string beans were on the menu for dinner. We sat down at the round, oak table. I stared for a moment at the hand-painted wallpaper and baskets of apples on a red, gingham tablecloth. I picked it out—something I still liked. Jimmy sang the grace:

"We thank thee God for food we eat,
For family and friends we meet,
For books we read and songs we sing,
We thank thee God for everything."

Then we made the sign of the cross. They didn't ask for their dad when his place was empty. I reached my limit tonight with Ray's behavior and waited until the kids were in bed. I took out my best china, heaped a mountain of potatoes in the center of Ray's plate and poured cold gravy on the top letting it run down the edges and pool at the base. Then I had a cigarette. It sizzled in the gravy when I put it out. I poked my next several butts into the sticky potatoes now resembling candles on a cake and dumped ashes on top of the pork chop as an afterthought—like adding powdered sugar or sprinkles. The folded napkin and fork were on the left. Knife, blade in, placed near the plate on the right. The spoon rested on the outside. I put tall tapered candles in a crystal holder and shut off the lights.

I was nearly asleep when Muffin, our mutt, yelped; I sat straight up in bed. Ray was home.

"Son-of-a-bitch, what are you doing in my way?" Ray slurred. I stood by the doorway and listened, and when the lights went on the dog tucked his tail between his legs and headed for Tori's room. Ray followed the dog and I bent over the railing now. He closed her door. I knew the sound of footsteps in my house. I could tell he was near. Shivers ran down my arms.

"Nice dinner!" he yelled, and headed for the basement.

Early in the morning, I cleaned up the mess, in slow motion. The kids sometimes thought that I was nuts but they didn't understand the impact of his constant drinking on our relationship.

Acting Out

It was Saturday. After tomato soup and tuna fish sandwiches, we finished chores. Jimmy took an armful of folded towels upstairs, and Tori carried her blouses and skirts on hangers to her room. Ray was sleeping on the couch in the midst of all this activity. His little bursts of whistles and snorts made the kids laugh, but I put my finger to my lips warning them to let him sleep, at least for now.

Ray didn't come to bed again last night and I have about had it with him. I harbored revenge, looking at him in wrinkled clothes and spittle. He looked like a bear with copious amounts of hair on his arms, chest and face. I undid the cord from the vacuum and plugged it in. I cleared my throat and made noises, giving him a chance to redeem himself, but he didn't move a muscle. I turned on the switch and the bag inflated. The faint light lit up a small section on the carpet, and a paper clip and small pebbles bounced and sucked up the chute. Ray still didn't stir. I lost control, ran the vacuum into the couch frame, and watched his face—but nothing. He reeked of cognac. He looked dead except the corners of his mouth were wet. I slammed the vacuum back and forth, all eight feet, and then banged it forcefully along the backside of the couch, since it was in the middle of the room.

The television blared, and I screamed, "Lunch is ready!" The kids stood open-mouthed on the stairs, and when I looked at them, they turned and ambled away, looking over their shoulders.

It was when I shut off the vacuum that Ray sat up and said, "What? Is there a problem?"

"It's time for lunch. We're waiting for you," I said and departed up the stairs.

I was still upset with Ray after dinner, so I scampered off to the grocery store, but strolled around like I had all the time in the world. Then I heard my name called out and looked across the meat counter at the wife of the man Ray got drunk with last night.

"Oh hi, Carol." We both smiled and then I asked, "Are you in the mood for revenge?"

"Sure, why not," she said and put her pound of hamburger back in the case.

"Up for a drink at the El Rancho Lounge?

"Great. I don't need groceries anyway—just getting out again." Even though we hardly knew each other, we looped arms like old friends and left the store.

The motel bar was full of men from the oil fields. Music from the '60s blasted through the sound system, and the more we drank, the prettier we thought we were. The guys sent rounds over and winked at us. We raised our glasses to thank them and had one Irish whiskey after another. I only spent one dollar the whole night, so Ray couldn't get mad about that. The overhead lights flashed the *'last call for drinks'* signal and the place started to empty. We kept looking at our watches. We couldn't leave until it was late enough to cause concern.

"Ladies, you'll have to leave now," said the now sexy-looking bartender.

I got in my car, rolled down the window for some fresh air, waved widely, tooted out Morse code on my horn and headed off in the opposite direction.

The streets were flat and straight, and I had one hill to go up until I pulled a little crooked into the driveway. I laughed uncontrollably in the yard. I tripped, said 'excuse me' to the step, and opened the back door. The lights were on downstairs. I tap danced *East Side, West Side* on the little rug at the entry so he knew I was home at this ungodly hour.

Ray yelled at top volume, "I don't know where you've been or what you've done, but you should do it more often!"

"Oh shit . . ." I mumbled over the toilet bowl.

Under My Roof

I volunteered to leave work at 4:00 a.m. because the census was unusually low. It was harder to work on a slow night than when it was crazy busy. I needed the break. For the twenty blocks to my house, streets were empty, the moon was creamy and it was like everyone in town was asleep. The word *peaceful* came to mind and I yawned, anxious to crawl into bed with my husband and get warm.

I took my shoes off, tiptoed into the house and headed to the bedrooms to check on the kids. Jimmy was asleep, his sock monkey hung off the side of his bed and the covers were up to his ears. I kissed his forehead, closed his door and headed downstairs. The bathroom light cast a shadow on our empty bed.

"Where are you Ray?" I whispered but no one answered.

Tori's bedroom door was open, so I peeked in at her sitting straight up in bed, with a blanket covering her small breasts. She was more frightened than I had ever seen her. . . Ray's naked body draped over her bare legs, asleep—his head on her flat belly. His white jockey shorts looked like he carefully stepped out of them, two underwear circles on the blue speckled carpet. *What the hell is going on?*

Tori's face flushed—eyes huge, dark and rounder than I remembered from the afternoon. I put my finger to my lips and tossed Tori a robe. Then, startled, he saw me and jumped from the bed to standing. I lunged, grabbed his shoulders, pulled at him, but Ray's sweaty body slipped from my grasp when he scooped up his shorts and covered his genitals.

"You don't understand," he said.

"You son-of-a-bitch—get out! I can see. Don't . . . don't even try to explain. Get your ass out of this house!"

"NO! I am not leaving. You *will* listen to me," he said, pinning me against the hallway closet. "You are overreacting to this whole thing. Pull yourself together. What's wrong with you?"

Loaded with adrenalin, I shoved him against the bathroom door but he spun out of my grasp and locked the door. I threw myself at the door and twisted the glass doorknob back and forth. My mind had difficulty believing what it saw. I marched back into Tori's room with a sinking heaviness in my feet—the kind that sucks your boots off in the mud. I went from seeing his shorts on the floor where Tori knelt for prayers, to her cheeks, burned pink from his beard, and my anger ran chills up my back and snapped my neck.

"Tori wrapped the blankets tightly around her entire body and turned herself to the wall. She pulled her foot away when I reached out to touch her.

"Tori, I'll take care of this." I closed her door.

I paced, moved around the kitchen, took small steps from the oven, to the table, to the sink, and back to the table. I grabbed a cigarette and lit it. I took two deep drags and set it in the ashtray. Then I lit one more. Noises like a wounded animal came from my insides and I wrung my hands. *I don't know what to do. Oh my God, help me . . . her own father?*

"Get out of this house," I screamed through the bathroom door.

"Cool off. I'll be right out and we can talk."

Ray came out from the bathroom straight for me and put me in a suffocating embrace.

"Let go of me," I yelled, swinging my arms. "Get out."

"If you will calm down, I will tell you what happened," he said.

"You can't say anything to make this better. I saw what I saw. I know what you did."

"No you don't! See . . . Tori was calling out for you. But you weren't here. She had a stomachache. I was getting out of the shower. She sounded so desperate I hurried into the bedroom before I had a chance to put my underwear on, and she wanted me to rub her stomach because it hurt. *Sooo*, that's all I did and I fell asleep. And that's that."

"Shut up . . . you're lying."

"Then ask Tori."

"I don't have to. I saw the look on her face."

"C'mon. Sleep on it. We can talk tomorrow. You look tired. Go to bed for Christ's sake."

"Not with you, asshole," I said and Ray headed downstairs.

I swallowed vomit and moved quickly back to Tori. My eyes, seared; my throat, bitterly parched. Tori's hand jerked up to her face as if to ward off a blow. I wrapped my arms around her quivering body and held her. I whispered into her thick, tousled hair where the scent of his cologne and cognac lingered. She fell asleep with me beside her.

~~~~

The next day, Ray refused to move out. He was bigger than I was and scary. I didn't know how to kick someone out of the house except to scream at them.

In the back of my mind, I could hear my mother saying to *me,* "Never leave a house or you will lose your house. The man leaves."

Today's Mail

It was odd that Ray stayed and our household was on its best behavior for the next whole month. It was hard to believe that something bad had happened. Ray came home after work in the late afternoon before the news, and we ate meals together with pleasant conversations—no more hanging out at the bars. Each day I prayed this happiness was real—what else was I supposed to do? The kids acted happy. Maybe it was over, but I knew I wouldn't forget what he had done.

Ray left town for a collectors show and planned to be gone for the weekend. This was the closest to normal that I had felt in a long time, and there were no worries when Ray was gone. In case of an emergency, I had my parents and a short sense of freedom. It was hard to miss someone who called often and asked what I was doing—and I'd report. Ray had this need to know exactly what the kids were doing and he talked to them. The conversations were short but, by the looks on their faces, he had said something they didn't want to hear or talk about when they hung up.

I was out in the yard when our mail carrier handed me a three-by-five package that read *"Do Not Bend."* I didn't recognize the return address, but I knew it was photos. I took them inside and ripped the strip off the cardboard envelope, leaned against the kitchen counter and examined them closer. The first picture was the family room in the basement. Tori was smiling . . . her braces shined . . . in that white dress I found in her room; followed by Tori in the same dress, only I could see through the dress and she was without underwear. Her slip and panties were on the floor next to her bare feet. I leaned harder against the red counter top. My mind moved so slowly, I was not sure I was still here. All the fears I had held back come crashing down. Without warning, there was a close-up of the top of her head, her light brown hair parted down the center, between Ray's pale hairy thighs—and another, and another, some with his fingers pressed on her mouth. Everything I had feared was proof in my hands. I couldn't close my mouth. I couldn't move. I folded each picture in half and then quarters. And I couldn't hear the back door open because of the roaring in my ears.

Tori stepped into the kitchen, arms loaded with dog-eared music books, a can of Dr. Pepper, a Three Musketeer bar and her purse hung from her forearm. She saw my face and knew what I had found.

"That bastard!" I screamed. "How could he do this?"

She pulled a chair out, let her books fall hard on the table and stared at me. I flashed on Tori being born, her first bath under the kitchen faucet and her Baptism . . . the first day of school and then that night when I came home early from work.

"He will never look at these! Never!" I screamed, "Tori, do you hear me?"

Her hands went to her mouth and two fingers covered her closed lips. I began ripping the pictures into unrecognizable shreds. And without realizing it, I had just destroyed all the physical evidence to prove a case. I muttered repeatedly, "*I hate you.*"

Tori dropped her candy bar, ran to her room and slammed her door.

Omigod, what had I said? "Wait. It's not you I hate . . . it's your father."

The Call

It was midnight in my hell. Ray usually called me again after the bars closed. My knees shook and bumped together, even when I put my feet flat on the floor. Nothing softened the sound of the pounding in my chest. I came downstairs and climbed on my exercise bike. I forced my feet to peddle. I didn't want Tori to hear me from her room, so I turned on music, and with the beat my arms flew and my legs pumped until the bike screamed a high-pitched hum, and I cried. I wiped snot on my sleeve and rode like I was actually getting the hell out of this family. I imagined it—my eyelids squeezed so tight I could only see red. The phone rang—my trance snapped. I picked it up before the second ring so it didn't wake the kids, but I didn't speak.

"Hello?" he slurred. "Honey?"

I held my breath and covered my mouth—afraid. I had never wanted to kill someone.

"Hello . . . What the hell is wrong with this phone?"

Then it went dead.

It rang again. I picked it up. "Don't come home," I said.

"What's the matter?"

"I found the pictures—in the mail!"

"What pictures?"

I remained silent with a lump the size of a boiled egg in my throat.

"You opened my mail?" he asked, with an edge to his voice. "Was it addressed to you?"

"Don't ever come home . . . it's over! I can't stomach the sight of you."

I slammed the phone down hard. I was as empty as a dry husk of an insect. If only someone could sweep me away. My long cry was unrecognizable to my ears.

After I took the kids to school the next morning, I began to tremble again because I saw Ray's car at the shop. I drove through the alley slowly, straining to notice if he had unpacked, and then continued past my parents' house and down our street. Even though I had grown up in this town, I didn't have contact with old friends. I had no one to talk to; I worked all the time, and they worked all the time. *What happens now?*

It was dinner time, and Ray made a lot of noise when he walked back into the house. He stomped his feet like he was kicking off dirt and put his clothes and briefcase away. I kept dusting the same furniture over and over while I watched him.

Firearms were located all over the house—on top of the

fridge, under our bed, in our top dresser drawer and in the front closet. "Guns," he had said, "are supposed to protect us from intruders." Ray concealed a small pistol around his ankle, tucked in his sock, when we traveled. But Ray was the intruder. The mere cleaning of them was threatening. My best bet was killing him with extra large amounts of food, specifically desserts. Murder was a mortal sin; his ass was saved because I didn't want to go to hell if it was anything like being here.

I listened, watched out of the corner of my eye and looked over my shoulder now. Being a nurse, I faced life and death every day in my workplace; I advocated for patients and stood up to doctors. But here in my own house, I didn't know how to debate or hold my ground with Ray.

At Ray's request, I sat down after the kids went off to school and faced him. He agreed we would get help when I insisted we go to therapy; so we called Information, got a phone number, called long distance, and ended up with an appointment in the neighboring state of Montana. Mr. Page, a licensed social worker, would see us in his satellite office, fifty miles away, on Saturday.

When Ray went to work, I sat alone with my thoughts. . . *No one can see us visit a shrink;* and, *Omigod, I need to protect my parents from any scandal.*

Therapy

The ride over was quiet, except for the normal amount of bickering in the back seat with the kids. I told them to behave and they nodded. Mr. Page met us in the parking lot outside his building, introduced himself and shook hands. He made a casual comment about who won the basketball game last night.

His office was next to the waiting room. First, we sat in front of him as a family, but Mr. Page didn't acknowledge our brokenness. He was too friendly. I wanted a police kind of person who would scare the hell out of Ray and threaten his life. The plan was to meet one at a time with him and then get back together at the end of the session as a family and talk.

Mr. Page called me in first. "Why are you here today?" he asked, like he didn't know.

"I already told you nicely on the phone, but I will say it again. I made this complaint because the asshole I married is messing with our daughter, and it's wrong."

"It has a name—*incest*," he said, sitting cross-legged in his wing-backed chair.

"Incest?"

"Yes. When a father . . ."

But I couldn't hear his words. I couldn't hold myself together anymore. I bent in half and rocked back and forth. Between sobs, I sputtered what I knew. "I thought that only happened to cults who inbreed, wear funny clothes and can't dance. I mean, they're not allowed to . . . and they can't wear lipstick or go to the movies—those people that still ride in a horse and buggy and make their own food. That's who does that . . . not my husband . . . not to our child."

"Excuse me," he said and left the room leaving the door wide open. He turned the radio up in the waiting room and glanced around. No one looked up at him. Ray was reading a book; Jimmy was mesmerized with the big goldfish in the tank and had no idea why we were here anyway, and Tori perused a teen magazine. He returned with a box of tissues.

Oh God, I was so confused. *How could he do this? The only thing that matches what I believe is that Ray has a beard like them. I've never liked his beard. Omigod, what am I going to do?*

Then Mr. Page said something one never expected to hear, "I'm really sorry. We aren't trained . . . I mean, I can't find anything about this in the books."

The corners of my mouth tasted salty and the collar on my blouse was soaked. I blew my nose, shoved the tissue into my sweater pocket and stared at him.

"Well, Mr. Page, exactly what am I to do?"

"Come back next week and we'll talk again."

"No, that's not good enough. How do I protect my daughter?"

"Has he done anything to your son?"

"I . . . I don't even know. That thought never entered my head."

"Well, tell me about your sleeping situation. I mean, what your house is like."

"Jimmy sleeps upstairs in a large room with slanted ceilings. Then downstairs our rooms are across from each other with the bathroom in between. Tori's room is the smaller one."

"Okay, now we're making progress. I want you to rearrange your bedrooms, the adults take the bedroom upstairs, and the kids can both be downstairs. They can watch out for each other. How does that sound?"

"Ray can easily walk downstairs, you know."

Mr. Page didn't move a muscle in his face. "That's it for now. See you again next week."

Tori got up when I came out and took my hand. She smiled with a mouth full of braces and I hugged her shoulders. She hugged me back and we marched arm in arm to the car. Her face was soft. I could tell she was different . . . maybe relieved. She chattered nervously about school and her new best friend. She smiled at me and squeezed my arm. That's what she did— squeezed my arm.

After Therapy

During the ride home, I tried to act normal—like it was over— because Ray promised. We were the typical American family with a boy and a girl and a house, a dog and two cars. I read *The Betsy* by Harold Robbins and paused between chapters to talk. Jimmy said he liked all the colors of the fish and that doing those puzzles was fun with Mr. Page, but now he wanted a hamburger. I wondered then if Ray had done anything to him. Tori said Mr.

Page enjoyed music and was interested in her music awards. And Ray didn't say a damn thing, only kept clearing his throat. He sucked on his cigarette and bit his twitching lip, looking straight ahead while his eyes shifted to Tori in the rear view mirror. It was midnight before we had finished switching rooms. The garbage can was full of clutter, like apple cores and candy wrappers from Jimmy's room. This was to be a fresh start.

Ray and I said goodnight and we each slept on our own side of the bed, with our legs flailing in our own spaces to warm our feet. In the morning when I awakened, he held my backside gently against his body. He said I was whimpering in my sleep, he wiped my tears with his fingers, and his lips pecked each bony knob up the curve of my neck under my hair. Minutes passed before the mattress eased and lifted as he got up from the bed. It was all betrayal and my empty gut held a crusty piece of hatred.

The next few weeks were like a test where I considered what I said with care and, with painful silence, watched every move Ray made.

I learned a word for Ray—*perpetrator.* That was what Mr. Page called him. Tori was the victim, and he didn't call me anything. She came home after school, practiced the piano for hours in the living room, and then we talked about her classes. Tori didn't know I had been in her room because I got good at being a snoop and didn't leave clues. I looked for signs that she might need my help. I looked for evidence that might be cause for concern and something I could confront Ray about. Jimmy, my meticulous budding artist, colored outside the lines and wrote cuss words on scraps of paper to attract more attention, so I spent more time with him trying to prove I was a good mother. We ate out a lot, but together attended Bingo on Thursdays at the school gym, went to Sunday Mass; and there, while I stood between Tori and Ray, told God that I thought my whole life was unimaginably unfair.

Mr. Page encouraged Tori to continue her music. He taught Jimmy the names of all the fish in the tank; and God only knows what he and Ray bullshitted about.

On our third and final family session, Ray nodded his head and said he would never harm either of his children. In conclusion, Mr. Page thought the relocation solution was successful. *Hell, I wasn't cured. I thought all daughters might be the objects of their father's desire.*

That Saturday, he shredded our records and considered us healed. We walked out together.

Mr. Page turned the lights out, locked the steel door, gave it a shake and said, "Looks like rain."

"Amen," said Ray and laughed like he said something funny.

Changes

Since therapy, I sneaked around my house more than before, and memorized every inch of it by heart, so I knew if anyone had moved, touched, or changed anything. Tori was harder to read because she withdrew from me, using school activities as the excuse. I was unable to resign my night shift without a replacement, and my supervisor wanted a reason; but I couldn't bring myself to tell anyone that I needed to be home at night to protect my daughter from her father.

I didn't know at that time that Ray lied about me, told the kids that we had to go see the therapist because I was the sick one, acting weird and being jealous of Tori getting so much attention. I didn't know that, *after* seeing Mr. Page, Ray had to cool off, and so he paid Tori to wait for him with a fifty-dollar bill. But Tori's relief was only short lived because he became more aggressive, picked her up at school and wanted her more often.

Ray became more imaginative and crafty—bought and bound her into his sickness. He wanted to marry her, and did, in his own ritualistic ceremony of promises so they could always be together, going so far as to threaten suicide if she betrayed him. Tori lied on purpose to protect me from the devastating truth, until she could get away from him.

I came home immediately from work—no accrued overtime. I hugged Tori when she awakened, smelled her hair and neck wanting to know if Ray had been in her room without asking. When he left for work, I checked the entire house for clues from the night before. I buried my nose in Tori's clothes for any lingering scent and put them back bunched up exactly the way I found them. I ran my hands across the sheets on her bed and left the same dents in her pillow. I stood in the middle of the room and turned slowly in a circle, glancing from floor to ceiling for anything. *I was afraid I was going to catch him again, but I first had to know that Tori was safe.*

~~~~

I approached slowly through the alley, shut the car off and sat behind Ray's store for a few seconds. If I used the back door, Ray couldn't see my car in advance and hide things. Then I came in and realized I didn't even know what I was doing. I yelled, "Hello," before I slipped into the bathroom and dug through his wastebasket. At the bottom were little scraps of paper. I folded each piece back the same way I found it and replaced them under the dead geraniums and coffee grounds. I scrubbed the sink and wrapped the cord around the vacuum cleaner to avoid any suspicions of loitering. Tori finished polishing a sterling silver bracelet from the front display case. Our argument was that Ray said he needed Tori more than I did. And he pushed it further, several months later, by asking to take the kids on a trip out of town.

"No," I said.

He tried to change my mind. "Tori's such a big help at the show—I need her."

"No," I said more emphatically.

Ray kissed me each time he left the house. He told me everyday that he loved me. This time he was going for a long weekend. I waved good-bye and smiled, relieved when his car pulled out of our driveway and Tori was still in her room.

One Sunday afternoon Tori and I took a ride out to Twin Lakes on the edge of town. I shut the car off and turned sideways behind the steering wheel to face her. First, I told her I loved her. The sun beat through the window and warmed my back. I smiled at her. It had been a long time since we had been alone.

"Is there . . . something you'd like to tell me?" I asked her.

Tori looked down at her hands and then out the window but didn't answer.

"Okay, is there something we can talk about?"

She shrugged her shoulders, but still no answer.

"I'm your mother . . . please talk to me, honey. I can help."

Tori rolled down the window. I swallowed hard.

"There's nothing to help."

Her lips pursed, her jaw locked and the muscles in her cheek quivered. When I touched her shoulder, she took such a deep breath her belly swelled and she exhaled loudly. I wanted to choke it out of her or scream at her, even run away with her, but she reassured me in a steady, calm voice, like she'd been coached.

"Stop frowning, Mom. Nothing is happening. I have to get home now and practice for my solo. Will you let me drive?"

I could never let my guard down. I searched, dug for evidence of sexual molestation all the time, and it drained me. She wasn't the same anymore. No more lacy dresses hung in her closet. Her baggy jeans, loose shirts and Converse tennis shoes disguised her slim body. When she cut her hair, it grew back unevenly, while mine cascaded to my elbows like *"Cher."*

Tori lied in a teasing voice about where she was going or where she had been. Her half-true stories about being late, filled with inaccuracies, sent doubt even further when she said, "I must have forgotten." I wanted to slap the condescending look off her face, but I let it go and told myself it would be okay. I would be okay . . . we would be okay.

Prom

Tori was going to Prom with her friend, Troy, whose father was my childhood neighbor. He came from a good family. She spent Friday afternoon with her girlfriend, and they gave each other French-tip manicures, pedicures, and rolled their hair. When Tori got home, she showered and I helped her finish getting ready. She was too excited to eat dinner and stayed in her robe until right before he arrived. Tori stepped into her peach, organdy gown, gathered at the bodice with ruffles, and I added my pearl necklace and earrings. She was tall. She weaved in her new high heels and switched back to white flats.

Ray sat in the kitchen waiting, glancing up at the front door with a half-empty glass. When the doorbell rang, I came out and answered it. Ray reared up from the table and steadied himself, leaning on the tall, ladder-back chair. He was intimidating, not only by his size, but by his large gold rings that looked more like brass knuckles.

"Come in," he yelled hoarsely in a smoker's voice.

Tori came around the corner, smiled and headed straight for the door. I touched her shoulder.

"Don't look like you're in such a big hurry," I whispered.

"I don't want Dad to embarrass us."

"I'll play interference. It'll be okay."

Troy handed Tori a small white box and she nervously opened it. Ray's booze breath spoiled my split-second dream of being a normal household. Troy slid the orchid over her wrist and Tori giggled. It was a perfect photo op, but I never ever wanted Ray to take another picture of Tori. I helped Tori pin the boutonnière on Troy's lapel and put Tori's shawl around her shoulders with a little, affectionate squeeze.

"Enjoy breakfast, but don't be too late," I whispered.

"Thanks, Mom."

"Stop," yelled Ray. "Bring her home right after the dance," Ray bellowed twice.

"Honey, Ray, all the kids go out for breakfast afterwards. It's what you do here."

"I don't give a damn. Tori, do you hear me? Home, right after the dance."

"Yes sir," Troy said, and Tori's face turned crimson. I hurried them along, waved my arms wide and bid them good night. The front door closed, and I peeked out the little window and watched Tori loop her arm through his, and I imagined the grand march, the balloons and the waxed floor.

Ray opened the refrigerator and took out a chunk of liverwurst and bread. He planted himself on the edge of the kitchen chair, leaned over the round table and mumbled, "That son-of-a-bitch better not put one hand on her, *or else*."

Ray returned to the kitchen at midnight.

It was 12:15 a.m. and I was still dressed. Ray's shirt hung off the back of the chair. The sound of the ice cubes dropping into his tumbler grated on me. He swished the cognac with his finger, sniffed his drink and sucked between his teeth before he swallowed. His eyes hung shut. I untangled my legs and stopped wagging my foot. The second hand on the clock moved too fast. Tori was already late and in trouble; now she might as well stay out even longer and enjoy herself.

"I'll wait up for Tori; you can go to bed," I said.

"No, I told that kid to bring her home after the dance."

"And I told them to go out and have a bite to eat with their friends."

"You what?"

"And they are probably having a good time."

At 12:30 a.m. a car backfired in front of the house. Right as Tori turned the knob, Ray pulled on it from the inside and she flew into the room, startled. She licked her lips. Her eyes were huge and she glanced over at me. In an instant, Ray gripped his hand around the back of her neck, clumsily shoving and dragging her into the kitchen. She whimpered.

"*Why didn't you call me*?!" he screamed at her, his red-veined eyes on fire.

I jumped between them and shoved them apart. He let go of her. Tori was now behind me her hands covering her mouth. Ray grabbed my shoulders, but I shrugged hard, took him by surprise and lunged at his hairy bare chest with knuckled fists. I struck hard enough to push him against the wall. He coughed and covered his heart. I pressed on his chin with the palm of my hand and looked straight into an old drunk's face. He smelled awful; gooey, white strings gathered in the corner of his mouth, and then he tried to bite me.

"Don't ever lay a hand on her again or I'll kill you," I muttered through gritted teeth.

Ray descended to the basement and slammed the door to his office. Tori rushed to her room and slammed her door, which had no lock. I followed her and opened the door slightly.

"Can I come in?"

"No; leave me alone."

"It's me—your dad is gone." I stepped in and faced Tori standing in the middle of the room. She took off her corsage, threw it on top of her books, and began to cry.

"I'm sorry," I whispered. When I put my arms around her, she pulled back stiffly.

"You said it would be okay. How come you didn't convince him—take care of it?"

I rubbed the back of her neck where his fingers remained etched and kissed the pink marks.

"But now look what I've done . . . Dad is so mad at me . . ."

"It's okay. He'll get over it sometime in his life," I said smiling now.

"We were having so much fun, and I didn't want to leave my friends."

"It's okay. I'm telling you—you didn't do anything wrong."

Mother's Short Visit

On the morning of the 15th, before I even opened my eyes, I knew I was alone in bed. *Where was Ray?* I threw on my chenille robe, and hurried down to the kitchen. *How long had he been up?* The toast popped at the same time Ray opened the back door carrying the empty garbage can.

"Good morning sleepyhead," he said, washing his hands at the sink.

"Good morning," I uttered. I leaned against the wall and watched. I wondered what he threw away. God, *I hated being so suspicious*. Ray whistled and poured a big beer glass full of milk. Scrambled eggs and jambalaya slid out of the frying pan onto his plate and he sprinkled hot sauce on every inch. I got myself a bowl of cereal and sat across from him. And we ate breakfast together. The kids had already left for school.

"I'm working in the bathroom. Don't be long—I need to get started."

"But my Mom's coming over this afternoon."

"So what?" he said, throwing his arm into the air.

"Well—nothing, I guess!"

My mother loved me and wanted the best for me. I called and we talked on the phone nearly every day, except when I made up excuses and skipped. I had to be excitably happy because she could read me and always knew when something was wrong. When Ray was around either of my parents, I worked especially hard at making it seem like we were happy and in love. It was easily recognizable that my Mom had that special something with my Dad, and I longed for the same thing.

~~~~

The sun filtered through the red curtains framing my bow window in the kitchen. Mom had black coffee and I had tea with cream and sugar. I sliced warmed brownies and served them and we licked frosting off our fingers, thumbed through magazines for new recipes and talked about decorating. It was a girlfriend kind of day, until Ray hollered and drowned out the soft background voice on the radio.

"*Get your ass in the bathroom and help me,*" he said.

A look of total disbelief covered Mother's face. I hesitated and grinned slightly, "Wait a minute, Mom."

"Now! I need you *now,*" he yelled. Ray was in the bathtub on his knees, in poor lighting and being dribbled on. I threw a towel down for him when the metal wrench hit the ceramic. "Fuck!" he screamed. Ray thrust his chin and gazed right into my face like I had made it happen.

I was embarrassed to tears and they spilled on his back and mixed with his sweat. I pointed towards the kitchen, mouthed the words, "Mom," and "*please.*"

"You stupid idiot! Can't you hold the flashlight still? This *god damn thing* won't hook right."

"*Then please, shut up!*" escaped through my gritted teeth. He lifted his head up facing the open door.

"I don't care if your mother can hear me or not. I want this damn thing fixed now." He twisted hard and after two more attempts and grunted, "Uuggghh! I've got it. Thanks sweetie," he said, tweaking my nose and patting my buttock. He sucked air through his teeth, lit up a cigarette, exhaled smoke in my face and said, "Now you can go back to your mother."

A bright flush covered my cheeks when I returned to the kitchen. I lifted my palm in front of my chest and splayed my fingers to shush Mom, who looked like a tiger ready to pounce. Anger and sadness blurred across her face, but she heeded my warning. She bit her lip and put her head down. It was no longer a hint—now Mom knew my struggle. I walked her to the door and said nothing. She kissed my cheek, squeezed my hand and left without saying good-bye to Ray. I knew she wouldn't tell Dad because it would upset him. Well, I thought I knew that, but it wasn't true.

Rained Out

As a family we attended parades, picnics and most of the community events. This year Ray joined a softball team, which surprised me because he was built more like a football player. The field was on the college campus a few blocks from our house. If the wind was right, you could hear yelling and beeping after a home run. I was unable to attend because of work. After the last game, Ray opened the trunk of the car and offered everyone a beer to celebrate and issued an "open house" invitation for a party. But the rain started, and people scattered before he could get a head- count.

Ray bought several bags of items from the store: chips and dip, beans, potato salad, buns and burgers, hot dogs, steaks and chocolate cake.

"Tomorrow, after the parade, we are having a huge party. Make a big mixture of daiquiris for the freezer and do one of your special salads—that crunchy overnight one—you know the one I like."

"Who's coming?"

"I don't know; maybe half the town," he laughed.

~~~~

We were ready. But it was drizzling and, even though the parade was canceled, Ray said that wouldn't stop anyone. One o'clock, two, three, four, five . . . I paced back and forth. He turned the music up so loud on his stereo, the floor vibrated. But, no one came—no one called. I was pissed, but I didn't know who at. I guessed we would eat this food for a week. When I opened the freezer to get a drink, there were gouged spoon marks riddled throughout the green shaved ice in the Tupperware.

"Hey, who's been in here?" I asked, but neither of the kids answered.

As the months flew by, life was comprised of *more* music lessons, *more* concerts *and more* sports. My night shift at the hospital and Ray's job at the store continued kept each of us occupied at least nine hours of the day plus the never-ending housework. Ray often helped but only under the pressure of the great inspectors, my parents, visiting. I was happy with the beds made and the dishes done.

The Nurses Convention

I drove with a friend to the annual State Nurses Convention, even though weather warnings and predicted storms suggested minimal travel, and only if necessary. I was the President of the local Association and represented my group. I looked forward to it each year, but this time I'd rather be home for those three days. And I explained that to Tori, but Ray convinced me that everything would be fine and I needed to go—so I did. It took longer than usual, but we arrived safe. We registered for the convention, checked into our rooms, looked over the program and had dinner.

Someone tapped me on the shoulder the next evening after the keynote address. I had a phone call.

"Mom," Tori said, crying, "everything's okay, but I'm so mad at Dad."

"Tori, what happened?"

"It's Dad—he's been drinking. He must have stumbled over the dog and fell through the glass cabinet in your bedroom. Blood and big pieces of glass are all over the floor."

"Omigod, are you all right?"

"I was so scared. I heard a thud and glass breaking, then a scream of cussing."

"Did he go into ER?"

"Yeah. I took him in and Dr. Kelly bandaged his arm. They did an x-ray, but nothing is broken. We were at the hospital for three hours. Dad got Vicodin and he's sleeping now."

"Tori, it's forty-nine below here. There are no more flights out tonight. Listen, I'll fly out early in the morning. Give your dad that old school bell in the pantry, and tell him to ring it if he needs anything. Otherwise, stay downstairs with Jimmy and leave him alone."

The Promise

When I got home, Ray promised to go to AA, asked me to trust him and said, "We can make our marriage work." He leaned over to hug me, but I couldn't bear to be touched.

The AA callback that evening was from a widowed man in our own neighborhood, who was immediately available. Ray invited me along to prove he was serious about cleaning up. We moved quickly through the bone-freezing drizzle two blocks down the street. I remembered this brown stucco house. I used to play there when I was a kid.

A sickish grease odor wafted through the air when he answered the doorbell. We shook hands in the small foyer and smiled at each other.

"Hello. I'm Bob, a recovering alcoholic."

"Hi. Well, I'm Ray and this is my wife. We live in the neighborhood."

"Welcome."

I couldn't tell how old Bob was from his weathered face and balding head. He walked like he was carrying a backpack of bricks. His gray pants had a monkey on the pocket and hung on his thin frame. In deerskin slippers, he shuffled to a screaming teakettle in the kitchen. A battleship puzzle with a thousand pieces sat on a card table. Yellow, floral bed sheets covered his old furniture. And the windows had been closed for a very long time.

"Why do you want to quit drinking?" Bob asked Ray.

"Well," Ray said, "it's really bugging my wife here."

"Is that the only reason?"

"Yup."

"Do you think you have a problem?"

"Nope, not really. I handle my booze fine. I told Emma I would do this for her, so let's get started."

Bob stared at Ray, nodded up and down, rubbed his nose back and forth with his pointer finger, and invited him to follow him. The two of them sat at the kitchen table under a bare light bulb, bent over steaming cups like two old friends and talked. Ray patted Bob on the shoulder and laughed a lot at him. Now they were both nodding—whatever that meant. I watched the small black and white television, caught smidgeons of this mutual admiration session, and when I looked down, realized my fingers were crossed. This old guy must have known that Ray's full of himself, and still when they finished, they embraced. I thanked Bob and hoped that their session would produce my miracle— that he'd stop drinking forever. I'd have to wait and see.

On the way home it was warmer, the stars filled the sky and the moon illuminated the manicured lawns. Ray tucked the twelve-step meeting schedule in his pocket and took my hand. Our palms rubbed together. He looked at me and smiled, pleased. I sighed as if I've been holding my breath all night. At least Ray talked to someone. Now I wasn't the only one who knew he had a problem drinking.

We passed the house on the corner with those pointy wrought iron swirls on the fence fitting for a graveyard. The air was crisp and fresh and an owl hooted. I didn't want words to ruin this new peacefulness. *Was Ray's drinking the whole reason he did bad things to Tori?*

Our dog was waiting in the yard when we got home. Ray held the door for me, and when I stepped into the house and removed my coat, his forearm grazed my breast. He closed in behind me and slipped his thigh between mine pressing gently. Then he nuzzled my hair and told me how good I smelled.

After a late dinner, I showered and shaved my legs. The kids were asleep, the lights downstairs were out and we headed up to our room. I stopped kneeling for night prayers a long, long time ago. Ray was under the covers smiling at me. It was my turn to shut the lights out, and when I saw Ray's shorts on the floor beside our bed, I had a Tori flashback lasting only a split second. And I wondered if it would ever be possible to have sex with him again. Ray nudged me in the small of my back with his middle finger. Obscene words screamed inside my skull. He wanted me to arouse him, but I scooted an arms length to the edge of our bed. I closed my eyes, stuffed my pillow into my gut and said I had cramps.

"But it's not that time of the month," he said and rolled over the other way.

His breathing changed from deep soft breaths to shorter, noisy ones. Sometimes it was longer than seven seconds before he exhaled. I turned over and looked at Ray's huge chest—a size forty-eight. One full day clean and sober, if you didn't count the codeine he took for a cluster headache after lunch. I slid my pillow back under my neck. Reflections from car headlights slowing down at the corner ran circles around the room. I repeated the Serenity Prayer in my head until my brain was hoarse, put my forearm over my eyes and drifted off.

Off to School

We were at home, eating dinner, when I knew that something was amiss during the meal. Yesterday Jimmy came into the house, walked around heavy-footed like he was still outdoors and Tori warned him. Now tonight, Tori corrected Jimmy for bad manners at the table.

Who told her to take over my responsibilities? Why does she think this is her job?

Ray chimed in with her, and the two of them acted like the parents.

"Tori, who died and made you the boss? That's not your job to correct your brother!"

She looked at her father as though he would correct me

and then hung her head, and in a whispered voice, apologized. I didn't understand what Tori thought about, and I wouldn't miss her bossiness.

The long sleeves of my cardigan kept the goose bumps away, and I folded my arms tightly under my breasts and gave myself a hug. I was a mixed bag of emotions. I was relieved knowing that Tori's school was far away from her father, who barely allowed her to breathe. I needed a break from the constant monitoring of Ray's activities. Tori's molestation stuck in my side, and I always looked for clues of more abuse. And someplace along the way, Tori grew up, was smart, talented and heading off to the University.

We shopped for new school clothes, a supply of nylons, sheet sets for a single bed, matching towels, a new pillow, an alarm clock and essentials for her make up kit. I sneaked little treats inside her suitcase of gum and candy bars. Ray packed the car for our trip in the morning. Jimmy stayed at his friend's house until we returned.

Ray hounded Tori with life lessons. He constantly questioned her with things like *What would you do if a car was coming straight at you . . . if someone grabbed your purse . . . if a boy touched you?* Then he told her why her ideas wouldn't work and gave her a better way. Ray was hell-bent on wanting her to know everything before she went away because he wouldn't be around to guide her. He sounded whiny when he talked about her leaving, and it sickened me. He acted like a lover was leaving—like he was being betrayed or something. He wasn't happy with her leaving, and I wasn't happy with her staying.

It was noon, eighty-five degrees and still, and we had only been on the road for two hours. Ray pulled off the two-lane highway and into Jake's Truck Stop. The screen door squeaked, then slammed behind us, but people barely looked up from their newspapers. We took the red, leather booth in the corner. I grabbed Tori's bare arm and pulled her to sit on my side so I could be close to her. Her eyes darted perpetually around the room.

The fans whipped above the tables like helicopters, and the red-faced cook wiped his damp forehead with the back of the sleeve of his white jacket, while Ray lit a fire on the end of his cigarette.

Tori and I had cheeseburgers, fries and vanilla shakes. Ray chewed his chicken-fried steak with mechanical precision and cleaned his plate of mashed potatoes and vegetables. It was uncomfortably quiet, so I begin to tell them how I liked living in the dormitory at Immaculata Hall. I chattered endlessly between sips of ice water and bites of food about what to expect at college. I was happy until my napkin slipped off my lap. When I bent down to retrieve it, I saw Ray's foot softly taping against Tori's shoe, and when I cleared my throat, she pulled her foot back. But Ray only stretched his leg out like a snake searching for its victim.

I said, "Good afternoon, Sister," and put the bags down beside the large brown desk. My heart beat loudly in this wonderful, structured environment. Sister examined Tori's admission papers, gave her a room number, a key, a map, a schedule and pointed to the elevator.

Two young women with fresh faces and big smiles were in the room to welcome Tori. Her new roommates introduced themselves and left us to say good-bye. But I wasn't in a hurry to leave. I liked it here and fought back the tears. I was already feeling empty; and now, I had lost her for good. But I moved through the emotions and smiled like a good mother.

One twin bed on the right and one bunk bed on the left, gray walls, three dressers, three desks and three bedside tables. Opening up the new sheets, I made up the lower bunk and put Tori's belongings in her drawer.

"Mom . . . Mom, it's okay. I can do this myself."

"I know . . . I know you can sweetheart. But I want to settle you in before we leave."

Together we hung all her clothes in her closet and lined up her boots and shoes. Ray took the suitcases to an assigned storage locker. Tori and I sat on the edge of the made-up bed, and she tossed her stuffed worn out bear up onto the pillow. I took both of her hands in mine and kissed them inside and out. Tori giggled like a little girl, and then we tearfully said good-bye. She hugged her dad who warned her to behave, shook his fist at her and winked. Then Ray took my hand and we left without looking back.

I blew my nose and crumpled the soaked tissue in my fist. I knew our life would change but I didn't know how exactly. Ray was too quiet. He cranked up the music in the car with a far away look on his face. Already there was the unspeakable void. In my wildest dreams, I didn't think things could get worse, but they did.

The Unexpected

While Tori was gone, Ray never mentioned her name. We attended Mass on Sundays and set up tables on Thursdays for Bingo in the school gym. I convinced myself that we were the ideal couple now. As time went on, I was almost convinced—at least in public places—that it was true. I stayed close by Ray's side, smiled, paid attention to him when he talked, and adjusted the collar on his shirt—the kinds of ordinary things I saw wives do in the movies. Ray gave me a peck on the cheek when the opportunity presented itself. But who was I kidding? The molestation of my daughter gnawed away in the back of my mind.

At home, if his eyes avoided mine, my face or my body, I made myself reach out and he responded. If I touched his arm, he put it around me and to his face; he kissed me. I put my leg next to his and it stirred some physical move—he always reciprocated.

I wanted Ray to attend Jimmy's functions at school, but suddenly, he became more preoccupied with work and left town for yet another show. Ray picked on Jimmy for no reason. He drank more now and stayed out later. I accumulated weeks of proof, marked on the calendar hanging next to the phone. I added red dots by each date he was drunk, and it looked like someone had bled all over the paper. I had enough ammo for a war, but I was playing solitaire. I don't know if this was a record of his drinking or of my misery.

Last year, Ray added a new storage space in the rafters of the converted garage, and I needed to make room for extra Christmas decorations. Innocently enough, I dragged the aluminum stepladder over to the wall, climbed to the top, stretched up and removed the opened padlock on the door. I pushed a heavy box too hard and it tipped spilling piles of pornographic magazines, each slippery cover sliding off the other and hitting the floor with a POW POW and POW sound. I scrambled to put them back, trying not to look at them and hurrying before Jimmy got home from school. In my rush, I closed the cupboard and clicked the padlock. If Ray discovered this, he'd know I knew the contents; so my plan was, if he noticed, to convince him he did it that night he had too much to drink.

When I mailed a letter to Tori early enough in the morning, it arrived at her school the same afternoon. She was four hours away, but it seemed like she was in another country.

I tucked the postcard invitation to Tori's concert back in with the bills. Tori said they were sent as a courtesy, and parents weren't really expected to drive from a long distance for that hour. Besides, Tori was so involved with her internship, we wouldn't have been able to spend much time together. I wished I could go by myself. I'd sit in the front row—the middle seat. I'd look at her, listen to her sing and play, and be filled with pride and satisfaction.

During dinner, I studied Ray's tired eyes and the creases in his forehead. His gray patches of hair made him look older than forty. He cleared his throat like he was about to make an announcement—and then he did.

"I have a buyers' show this weekend, out of state."

"And . . . so?" I passed him the meatloaf.

"It'll be the same 'pack, unpack, repack and load up the stuff' that bores you. I don't need you to go with me this time," Ray said, "And you deserve a break."

"Oh, thanks," I bowed to him.

He laughed, "I have lots of catching up to do around the house."

Then Ray perked up and kissed me. He held my face in his hands and gave me that promissory kiss of his, ran his fingers through my soft, long hair and tilted my face up to his.

"But not now," he said, pushing my forearms down to my side and backing up.

"Unh-unh, Ray," I said. "Don't stop now . . ."

"When I leave, I want you to want me . . . and you will like it when I come back; trust me."

Trust? I snapped back as if a wasp had stung me, *not in a thousand years*.

"I'm going to the store to load the car, so don't wait up for me," he walked away and turned around quickly, strutting back to put his lips perfunctorily on mine. We carried out this ritual of never parting without kissing good-bye—no matter where we were. It was the only thing in our marriage that hadn't changed. And we did it because that's what we did. It was our thing—like my parents.

The morning was chilly. The wind nearly pulled the screen door out of my hand when Ray backed out the driveway, then I let Mom know I was free for lunch. After Mother asked me about Ray's whereabouts, I realized I didn't know exactly where he had gone. I made up a place and kicked myself for not getting the particulars. Ray didn't even tell me. *How did that happen?* I had let my guard down since Tori left and concentrated on Ray's drinking. All weekend I left messages for Tori on the hall phone with her roommates: *"How was the concert?"*. . . *"Was there a good turnout?"*. . . *"Was it fun?"*. . . *"I'm sorry I couldn't be with you."* But I never heard back from her.

~~~~

Now it was the beginning of a new week, and the shadows from the streetlight danced on the slanted ceiling. *Where was Ray?* My lids were heavy, but I was awake—waiting and exhausted from the anticipation of his homecoming. He loved my seductive scent of perfume and the feel of black satin. I dropped off until the wind whipped the curtains straight out from the window. Startled, I slammed the window closed and watched lightening crack and zigzag in the sky. The thunder rolled like a bowling ball down an alley, and then dead silence.

When the phone rang at two in the morning, it was Ray. Car trouble again—it would be another day and a half. Then he added, "Tori says hello," and immediately disconnected.

I held the dead phone at arms length and screamed, "You bastard!"

November 1984—My Cry for Help

It was difficult finding a time to shop and hard getting excited about Thanksgiving. Ray's drunkenness and my loneliness were an unbearable combination. Tori was at college and he was unhappy and sulked, unless leaving town for a buy and sell show in the neighboring tri-state area. When he was out of town, he called each night. He asked me for a rundown of exactly what I had done all day, who I had talked to, and how Jimmy had behaved. Ray cared more about us when he was away than when at home. When he called me a "true blue, white side-walled, chrome-plated basket case," he thought I was a perfect so-and-so.

I was grateful that my job was a pleasant distraction from my personal life. The staff and my patients liked and respected me.

I finished up with my last patient, completed my charting and said good night to the housekeeper, who was the only other person left in the clinic. I put my nurse's cap in the cabinet and headed for the break room. I lit up and blew the smoke away, clearing my thoughts. I knew I couldn't take Ray's drinking any more. I smashed the butt in the clean ashtray, took a seat under the wall phone, and dialed the crumpled number I'd carried around in my pocket for weeks.

"Human Resources Center. Can I help you?"

"Yes. I need help right away."

"Are you in physical danger or thinking of killing yourself?"

"No and no." I emphasized.

"What's the matter then?"

"I'm a nurse. Please, it's personal. I have to see someone. When I arrive, I'll still be in my uniform; I'd like you to wave me in immediately. I can't sit in your waiting room. I don't want anyone to see me."

"Well we have a questionnaire you have to fill out first. Have you been here before?"

"Can I talk to your supervisor?"

"She's in a meeting, but hang on a minute."

I was on hold with a sickening love song and waited. "Come in, Ma'am. Someone will see you."

I parked at the far end of the block, down from the main entrance. The brass plaque that used to say Mercy Hospital on First Avenue was no longer visible. Now the familiar two-story, brick building was office space for the mental health services and retirement apartments.

I was born a middle child here at Mercy Hospital—four years after my brother and seven years before my little sister. And my grandmother died in Room 320. When Mother had a hysterectomy, Dad told people it was pneumonia. My father had his gallbladder removed in Room 312, directly across from the elevator. His stones were still in a jar in their bathroom. My brother had a ruptured appendix, and his room adjoined a sun room where Mom stayed overnight. My sister gave up her tonsils here too. And I had warmed a few beds with the Asian flu in '55, pneumonia in '58 and hepatitis in '65. I loved this ghostly place.

I recalled in an instant the smell of steamed sheets from the laundry, the taste of the warm, lumpy oatmeal from the cafeteria, and the rustling of the nun's long habits, as they hurried down the hallway. They seemed to dash in and out of closed doors that held secrets about God. My yellow autograph dog, signed by all the people who took care of me here in the fifth grade, was still in the front of my cabinet. I worked there all summer after my graduation.

The wind blew over the trampled snow and drifted along the street forming icy crusts. Chilled, shaking and very determined, I stomped my nurses' shoes on the mat before going into the lobby. My white uniform was visible under my coat.

The receptionist mouthed, "She's here," stepped out, and met me halfway. We walked down a narrow hall into a small room with two leather chairs, a dark stained desk, and a macramé hanging planter with fake greenery. "Someone will be with you shortly."

"Thank you," I said keeping my professional face.

In only a few minutes, slush formed beneath my chair from my shoes and when I got down on my knees in my uniform to wipe up the mess with tissues, the door opened. I apologized to a tall woman with snowflakes melting in her hair and green eyes. Her a-line skirt, cashmere sweater and black-heeled boots were impressive.

"Hi. I think I've seen you before. Do I know you?" I said.

"No, we've not officially met, but I've been watching you for a couple of years."

"Watching me?"

"Actually, I've been waiting to meet you," she said, extending her hand. "Have a seat, please."

"Not just you—your whole family—for the past two years."

I leaned forward, curious, not understanding what she meant and then she explained.

"I divorced my husband and moved here with my children for a fresh start." She continued, "Whenever I see you in Mass . . . well, your husband; I can't take my eyes off him."

"My husband drinks too much and it's awful. I can't pretend anymore that nothing is wrong. Please help me." I begged.

"My ex could be his identical twin. This is alcoholism—a family disease. We each play a role. I'd like to help you."

"You know about this?"

"Yes. And like I said, I've been waiting for you."

"I'm not crazy?" I sobbed.

"You're not." She handed me tissues. "I'm so glad you're here.

The next two hours flew while I soaked up compassion and validation. She hugged me, and we scheduled an appointment to include the kids. We initiated a plan for an in-house treatment intervention for Ray. He would be furious and I didn't care. This was my first secret from him, and my stamina was back.

The wind gusts rocked the car while I waited for the windows to defrost. My teeth chattered and I chanted, "I'm not crazy. I'm really not crazy. It's just a crazy feeling." The heater blew lukewarm air in my face now. It was getting dark. The moon was a chalky white. My tires crunched over the sunken tracks in the lot and I was hopeful. Two blocks away, I stopped at the corner market and picked up a Supreme Garbage Wagon Pizza with sodas to celebrate. I dared not tell anyone why. I couldn't afford to jinx the only possible chance of keeping this family together.

The Plan

As soon as Tori came home for vacation from college, we had a meeting behind Ray's back with the counselor.

Jimmy, Tori and I sat staring at each other with our homework from the counselor in the back of a half-empty A & W. We waited for our cheeseburgers and root beer floats along with some kind of divine intervention.

I placed three ballpoint pens in the middle of the table like weapons. It was difficult for Jimmy to handle serious matters, so he lifted his left cheek off the bench and made a loud snort. Then he giggled and let another one ripple.

"That's gross, Jimmy, go to the bathroom," I said.

"Oh *P.U.!*" Tori said. His brown hair looked like the scruffy grass that grew beneath our pine tree. Tori left him and slid over to my side of the booth.

"Why do we have to tell Dad all the bad things?" asked Jimmy.

"Because we're going to help him get better."

The counselor told us to look right at his face and say clearly, "When you did this, I felt that."

"But he's gonna be mad. I don't think he drinks *that* much," mumbled Jimmy.

"Yeah well, you're a little kid, and you miss stuff."

"Shut up Tori! I've seen things." Jimmy licked his finger and rubbed it across his right eyebrow.

"Stop it—both of you. Nothing bad will happen, *if* we stick together. Your dad will pick apart the weakest one. So that's why we're going to be ready. We need a good plan."

"How does this help Dad?" said Jimmy.

"Jimmy, when you stand with your friends in *Red Rover, Red Rover* and loop arms tight, no one can get through, right?"

"Yeah," Jimmy said.

"Well, this is done with words instead of arms. So write something down."

"But I hate this. I don't want to be here."

"Does he get to see our list?" asked Tori.

"Never. It's your cheat sheet."

"Can I draw pictures?" said Jimmy.

"Mom," Tori said, "your napkin is already covered in ink."

"Yup, I'm mad. I'm damn mad. I want him to get better. I want our family back. Tori . . . stop folding and get writing. You must have lots to say."

"Mom, I called you two weeks ago," she said with passion. "I told you Dad was an alcoholic. He does everything they say alcoholics do—and more."

Tori glared at me so intensely her eyeballs shivered. She tossed her hair and dismissed me. I stared back.

"Yes. That's what this is all about, Tori—his drinking and *nothing* else. We all have to say what we hate about his drinking."

"But Mom . . ."

"Okay, I'm trying to be clear here, Tori. What upsets you about your dad's *drinking*?"

"*You* upset me!"

"Watch it, Tori."

Tori moved to another booth and sulked. She looked pale and sat round-shouldered, with gray sweats hanging on her lean body. You couldn't see her breasts or curvy hips. Converse high-tops hid her long, narrow feet and ankles. I vividly remembered my little Tori in her favorite brown plaid dress, with yellow satin bows in her hair. I remembered the times as a baby she cooed with her bottle and when I comforted her with rocking and a song. I remembered when she couldn't say her *r*'s and called bread "*bledd.*" Tori had a stack of scribbled napkins in front of her and bits of torn paper.

"I can't think. This is stupid. I hate Dad right now." Tori kept her heavy-lidded eyes downcast. She clenched her teeth and her cheek pulsed like I've seen Ray's do when he was angry.

I reached over and stroked her shoulder. "Really, I'm sorry," I said, but she pulled away. I was scared too, and said I wouldn't let the secret we held come out to hurt her—not now. "Tori, I'm going to protect you. You can sit right next to me and we speak only with permission. You'll see."

"Sure Mom. We tell Dad he's an asshole and get away with it."

"Tori, that's enough. Act like you're in college."

She sneered and I turned away from her.

Eventually I knew what happened to Tori as a young child would come out. I thought about what Ray did to Tori every time I was with her. And I really thought things would be better once she was out of the house, away at school.

I suspected Ray was probably having an affair because sex happened once a month or maybe two times. And I had changed deodorants, nightgowns, and dotted myself with expensive perfumes, but things weren't better. I was on edge, ready to blow up at Ray—over Tori first, and the booze, missed workdays, broken promises, unfinished jobs around the house, and whatever else wasn't right. I thought Ray was too persuasive—that he might get away with everything. No one had ever dared confront him. Ray did whatever he wanted to do.

What if we didn't get him to commit to change? And then he knew exactly what we thought of him.

After dessert and a cigarette, I suggested we practice aloud once. "Each one of us gets to say what bothers us. No one else can hear us."

Jimmy showed us a picture of a dog and said he hated it when his dad kicked the dog, said it was scary when Ray got mad at him or raised his voice. But most of all, Jimmy hated his smelly breath. We agreed and applauded with our fingertips so as not to draw attention to ourselves. Tori said he made her late for school and rehearsals and embarrassed her in front of her friends, by flirting with them and acting like he was one of them. Again, we finger applauded. And Tori smiled. I followed that with how much I hated covering up for him, making excuses, listening to lies and living with a drunk.

I slapped my hand flat in the center of the tabletop. Jimmy followed suit, placing his on top of mine. Tori added hers, then mine, then Jimmy's, then Tori's again. We kept our hands stacked like a tower while I gave my pep talk. "I love you kids. What do you say? Can we do this?"

"We can do this," we chanted, and gently slipped our warmed hands out from the pile one at a time. Their sweet faces were soft, cheeks pinked, eyes widened and their exhausted toothy grins made me laugh. We left the restaurant with the events of our afternoon sworn to secrecy.

I stood on the staircase, jammed my knuckles against my

mouth and prayed that what I was about to say would work. Then I approached Ray, sitting at the kitchen table with his back to me. I planted lipstick kisses on the strawberry birthmark on his clean-shaven neck. He tipped his head back and made a soft noise. My heartbeat quickened and I kissed his ear. He pulled out the chair for me to sit down and smiled. I invited him to meet a counselor from our church who was going to help me, and Ray agreed. And the trap was set.

The Intervention

After introductions, Jimmy, Tori and I sat in a semicircle facing Ray. The counselor looked stunning in her navy silk suit and heels and used that strength of beauty to keep his attention. She thanked him for coming and offered him coffee or a soda. He declined and so she continued talking and set up the ground rules.

He knew then that he'd been tricked. We looked directly at him like we had been coached, and Ray's reaction was a long piercing glare, first at Tori then, turning his head, aimed his eyes at Jimmy, who wiggled a bit in his chair, and last at me, hiding behind my well-practiced stone-face. Then he put his hand on the chair to stand and the counselor lobbed the bomb. She told Ray to sit back down, that he had a loving family that wanted to see him get healthy. He stiffened and frowned, biting at his short, graying mustache. He was outnumbered.

Ray reminded me of a mad dog, a big dog, with his tail down, snarling and seething, ready to bite each of us, barking silently and fuming. I clasped my hands on my lap so he couldn't see them trembling. We kept looking at him, and when Ray cleared his throat, it wasn't threatening. But with strong voices, we began our unwavering first hour litany: *When you did this, this is how it felt.*

The counselor kept us on track. When Ray opened his mouth and wanted to speak, she told him to listen. At the end of each of our lists, we added that we loved him and wanted him to get better. He had no defense.

We didn't take a break, and in the second hour, I got a tissue from the box on the floor. Ray sweat, drummed his fingers, shuffled his feet and contorted his pale face. I saw a hidden vulnerable side of him. Ray, given only a limited amount of time to speak, was to talk only about himself. We didn't respond. We all kept straight faces so he couldn't read us; and for the first time, I saw how strong Tori, Jimmy and I were when we united. Silence between the confrontations, the heavy air smothering us and then sighs, while we waited for his response to our request.

Ray finally agreed to go to an in-house, thirty-day treatment program, but he insisted on holding off until after Christmas. He needed this holiday show. It was where he made most of his money for his business. The counselor accepted his reason and made reservations for the first of the year. Ray, who always got the last word, said nothing when he walked out the door. He left alone. The counselor hugged us and said our intervention was successful. However, I wouldn't be happy until he was clean and sober.

The next day, Ray sat at the kitchen table with his head in his hands. He ran his fingers through his thick hair and pressed on his skull. He was having one of his unpredictable cluster headaches. I learned to stay out of his way. He was agitated. His clenched fist meant he wanted to hit something because the pain was too much to handle. He put a pill under his tongue, rubbed Tiger Balm ointment on his temples and moaned. The toothpick container spilled on the Formica counter. Ray, his near lipless mouth pulled open, looked wild with toothpicks jutting out between his teeth. I ran cold water over a small washcloth, put it on the table, and darkened the room before I left.

Even though Ray was upset with me for tricking him, he wasn't upset with the kids, which meant to me that he didn't see us as a team. Again, he split us up. It wasn't a spoken directive or anything like that—it was a silent undermining—but he'd still have to go to treatment. We slept in the same bed, but Ray distanced himself from me. Still, in spite of everything that had happened, Ray told me every day that he loved me. He told me every day that I was beautiful. I was mad at myself for feeling compassion for his physical pain.

Merry Christmas

It was our nineteenth Christmas Eve together, and I traditionally made my famous oyster stew. Platters of prawns, cheeses and crackers, baked breads and condiments filled the table. The chocolate fudge, white divinity and popcorn cakes sat in the festive bay window with peppermint sticks and bowls of candy beside a huge poinsettia from the clinic. The real turkey and trimmings were happening tomorrow at Mom's house.

Tonight Mother and Dad were here. They came every year when we opened presents. Christmas music played in the background. Dad got an engraved pocketknife, and Mom got a religious statue for the bedroom. Ray opened his gift—it was a huge decorated box and all he had to do was lift it off and reveal a beautiful solid wood office chair that swiveled. I had saved up for it. Ray pulled my gift all the way out from behind the tree. I wondered how a grandfather clock could be so skinny, but maybe that was just one section. Ray was full of surprises.

Everyone stopped opening gifts to watch me peel the shiny red paper off the box. I put the white and green bows in the *"use again next year"* bag. I laughingly pulled at these legs and then when they were out of the box, much to my surprise, my gift was a metal ironing board with a shiny silver pad included. *What?*

Ray smiled and sat in his new chair.

"Thank you," I said politely. *Touché!* I had just experienced something unexpected, *as unexpected as his intervention into treatment*? He drenched me in revenge.

Poor Mother fiddled with the ribbon on her package pulling and releasing the curls. She felt sorry for me and sort of wagged her head. I hated that. But she didn't know what this was all about. The kids looked at one another and then at me with raised eyebrows and continued opening their presents.

"Excuse me. I have to go to the kitchen and check on something." My heated face was going to give me away. Pity tugged at me like a little kid and remembered every disappointing Christmas. It was Christmas—I gave him a nice present. I thought he was mean and my heart and my stomach hurt. I drank two glasses of water, checked the mirror and smiled hard, so it would stick. I swallowed the lump and got my voice under control but stayed quiet. I carried a big plastic garbage bag downstairs to collect the gift wrappings off the floor.

When we completed the unwrapping, Ray crawled way under the tree and brought out two more gifts for the kids. Most of their gifts had been of necessity—new shoes and clothes and jackets and boots. Ray acted as if it was just the three of them now, even though Mom, Dad and I were sitting right there. Jimmy whooped and danced when he got a wooden box complete with expensive art supplies. Tori opened a stunning gold watch and her mouth dropped in surprise. We got hugs as they were delighted with their wonderful gifts, but I didn't know about them in advance.

I worked hard and paid the mortgage and *all* the bills with my check from the hospital. Ray put his money into the business and seemed to buy the best of whatever he wanted to have. *Touché again*.

I wondered how many times I could die inside before it actually killed me. *If I were a cat, I'd be dead by now*.

Happy New Year – 1985

Christmas was over, our shop closed for a month and our Lincoln Continental was in the driveway. The trunk held Ray's suitcase alongside Tori's bag, as well as extra blankets, candy bars and emergency equipment like flashlights, batteries, and matches. It was time for Jimmy and me to say good-bye to both of them.

A cigarette burned in my right hand that I didn't recall lighting. I paced through each room of the house, glanced around like one does when leaving a hotel room, and made sure they had whatever they needed. The cold air that blew through the slightly-open door went up my dress and chilled my body as I watched Ray's every movement. He would be a different man after treatment and this excited me—to think about him without booze. He leaned forward, reached his large hands across the windshield, and shaved off thick strips of frost with a blade. He kicked his boots against the lower step, dropped chunks of ice off his soles and yelled for Tori.

Ray and I made this plan: Tori would go with her dad, drop him off at the treatment center and head out seven miles to her dormitory at the college. The whole trip would only take four hours. Tori would keep the car for the month. I didn't really like this idea, but I didn't have a better one.

Ray stepped inside, his whole body filling the doorway, squishing Jimmy until he laughed and yelled *"uncle."* The fresh snow covered Ray's beard and melted on his lips. Our mouths fit together perfectly for a long good-bye kiss until Jimmy said, *"Yuk."* Then Ray put an almost too heavy hand on my shoulder.

"Stay inside so you don't catch cold," he said. He licked his sandy-gray mustache, bit his lower lip and chewed on the little patch of stiff hair below it. For a split second, a panic of loneliness swept over me. A scared voice screamed *please don't leave!* but no one else could hear it inside my head

Are you okay, Mom?" Jimmy asked.

"Yes, honey. I'm fine."

I recognized my churning gut as the wrenching fear I had of Ray being alone with Tori, having him talk her into something, doing something sexual with her. I hated them going off together. Forever scorched into my brain was Ray jumping up from her bed, swooping his undershorts off the floor. I was scared for her. I didn't trust him.

I pulled Tori into me and told her I loved her. She patted my back seriously, like an adult to a child, the *"not to worry"* or *"it'll be okay"* pat, then she hugged Jimmy. She looked older today.

"Call more," I said.

For a long, grave moment no one spoke. Tori put her care package of goodies next to a brown sack with extra cookies and sandwiches for the trip. I waved as though they saw me, but clouds of exhaust surrounded the windshield when they backed down the driveway.

I thought positively and looked forward to a great year, especially with Ray off to a residential treatment center, and I resigned to take better care of myself.

I walked into the local furniture store on Broadway and First Street and purchased a tall, cherry Colonial Grandfather Clock with a golden face. I refused to get my husband's signature and said I would make all the payments. The payment book mailed to my house established for the first time credit for me as a woman. I made every payment on time and told the kids it was my *freedom clock,* which stood for way more than they could imagine. And today it stands to remind me, as the song says, "I am woman!"

It was unusually peaceful around the house with just Jimmy and the dog. Ray wasn't allowed to call home from the treatment center, so I had a break from his excuses and bullshit.

The wilted Christmas decorations came down. I purposefully focused on each task, rearranged the furniture and cleaned like company was coming. I attended Al-Anon every night, made new friends and spent hours over at my sponsor's house having coffee and lengthy discussions about the steps, hopes, fears and God. Jimmy and her kids played board games and watched movies. Karen was married, but her husband worked the oil fields in Alaska and was home one week out of each month. I became hopeful and relieved for the next two weeks because her strengths supported me.

The Call

I washed two plates and two glasses before the phone rang. I threw the damp towel over my shoulder and answered.

"Mommmm?"

"What's the matter Tori? Are you sick? What's wrong?"

"Mom, I can't go to Family Week with you."

"Well, you have to and that's that."

"I can't go Mom. Listen to me. I can't go!"

"NO Tori. You listen to me. I'm your mother! I'm telling you what you are going to do and that's it. Do you hear me? It's settled. Do you hear me?"

"Yes, but I won't be there. I'm sorry Mom . . ."

"Sorry about what?" I stared at the heavy wet snow in the old sandbox in the backyard. Even that looked fresh to me and I wanted a fresh start.

"I'm trying to tell you something . . . will you listen?"

"Okay Tori. Tell me."

"It's not that easy. Are you sitting down? Sit down Mom."

I grabbed an ashtray, lit up the last half of a cigarette and stretched the telephone cord over the chair.

"All right; now, what is it?" I could hear her breathing and I waited. *This had better be good.*

My scratch pad was in front of me; I doodled but was ready to write down all the bitter arguments—reasons I thought I knew about why none of us wanted to go to the treatment center or talk to Ray until he was well.

"MOM, IT NEVER STOPPED!" she screamed and then began sobbing.

I could hardly take in her tangled words, and when I jumped from my chair and tried to stand, it was difficult. I sunk my teeth into my number two pencil, picked up another, snapping it in the middle like it was a tiny twig. Then I made the sign of the cross repeatedly wondering how God let this happen to one of my babies?

"Tori . . . Tori, I'm so sorry."

"Mom, I couldn't stop him. I tried once but he threatened to hurt you and Jimmy. I'm sorry, Mom." Then it was quiet on the line. Dead quiet.

God, what did all this mean? God, God . . . I asked you a question. Till death do we part?

It can't work. I married for better or for worse but, this . . . was beyond worse, Help me!

Tori didn't have to tell me more. I knew she was telling the truth I was never able to uncover. I shivered; the blood drained from my cold face to my feet planting me in the chair.

Seconds later an adrenalin load hit and my pulse leapt in my chest with a jolt. I stood up balanced, straight, and taller than I had ever been, elongated my neck, and lifted my chin. I dried my tears and focused on a spot on the church calendar above the phone. There was no dribble to my sounds. My voice was now unrecognizably strong.

"Mom," she continued, "we were eating dinner and Dad said, 'Jimmy, leave the table and stay in the bathroom until you can wipe that stupid look off your face.' Then Dad kicked his butt with the bottom of his shoe, humiliating him. Then he demanded *you* stay in your place, and he held your arm down by your plate."

I remembered with alarming clarity. But of course, back then, I couldn't figure out what it was all about. "Oh God! I was so stupid. Tori, I'm sorry."

"Mom . . . Mom, are you mad at me?"

"No, I'm not mad at you. Thank you, for finally telling me."

"Someday I'll tell you everything, Mom, but I can't . . . not now."

What Else Is Going On . . .?

I went downstairs to the basement to look in Ray's office. He knew if anyone entered or touched his things, because he placed invisible tape and clear fishing line across the doorways. Tonight, I didn't care and inserted the hidden spare key into the lock. Boarded windows made it feel like a chilly black hole. I smelled his cologne and stopped, waited, for just a second because my stomach quivered. I counted to ten and told myself, if nothing happened by then, I was safe. I slid my fingers slowly down the cold, dimpled cement wall. The switch was behind the metal bracket that held up a long shelf. Something fell on the floor and broke. *Oh shit*. My heart pounded in my ears.

The first things I saw to my left were statues of Jesus, Mary, Joseph and the angels in an antique box that belonged to his dead grandmother. I shook my head inside this nightmarish room. I stepped over a pile of boxes on the floor and shoved a stack of books out of the way. His Knights of Columbus sword hung on the wall. Boxes of illegal fireworks sat beneath the second desk. My tears splashed onto a tray holding unfiled tax returns.

Then, with my lips pressed tightly together, I sucked in air and rooted through papers, conscious of my staccato breath. I dug into boxes containing small collectible art pieces. I dumped a tin filled with motel room keys. I lit one cigarette after another; the butts burned down to the filter and filled his ashtray. A dog barked outside in our yard, and I heard muffled voices and froze until it was quiet again.

Razor blades, mirrors and disassembled ballpoint pens were on the ink stained liner in his desk drawer. Shaking, I nearly cut myself when I rummaged through broken glass and blades in an old cigar box. Then I matched the blue bottoms with the blue tops and the black ones and yellow ones and brown ones the same way. *I should be able to manage this mess; after all, I work with life and death everyday. And why in the hell did Ray do this to good pens?* The little springs slid over the stems, and I clicked each one and tried it out. They were from the local bank, our insurance company, the hardware store, several bars and out of town hotel rooms. I pocketed two red ink pens I could use for the night shift at work, took one of them, and scribbled on a pad of paper. *How could you* . . . I wrote and crossed out. *You son of a bitch* . . . I wrote and crossed out. *You bastard* . . . again, I dug the pen into the paper until it cut into the finish on his desk. "I hate you," I said and realized I was screaming.

Next, I uncovered dog-eared Polaroid pictures taken in our house in Utah. I was pregnant with Tori at a limbo party. I remembered now. 1966. It was *Sexy Sue* they called her—pleated skirt, parted legs and lace panties. Then I saw his old high school sweetheart in her poodle skirt and a class picture of my little sister. I stuffed my sister's picture into my pocket and threw out a checkbook from a bank I didn't recognize.

Suddenly it was clear to me why Ray was different from anyone else I knew. He looked at *all* females sexually—whether he was drunk or sober—sick like that man in town who smelled women's underwear on the clothesline. Who was this father of my children? I didn't know him. This kept getting worse. How much could I take? I stood with my legs together and my stomach pulled in so tight it nearly touched my spine, shivering. I lit up another cigarette, opened a can of coke, and dug some more.

A silver metal box attached to the wall had a short cord running through a hole into the hall closet. The door jammed. I worked hard moving things out of the way and got it open. Bundles of magazines were behind the two-by-fours. I pulled one out—close ups of hermaphrodite genitalia. Nothing about the sick son-of-a-bitch shocked me now.

I got on my knees and followed the cord up the wall where three cables bunched together. I reached up to the top shelf to more cables and camera equipment. I gave the cords a tug, but they didn't budge. I stood on a step stool. One of the lines trailed across under the ceiling panels. This must have had something to do with how he knew everything that happened in our house. I kept searching for more. I forgot to swallow and choked, thinking how I never dared offend him.

Under a pile of papers were a solid red light and a blinking green light on a machine no bigger than my tape recorder. I didn't even care if it was a bomb. I pushed the center button. It was my mother's voice from our last phone call, then Tori chatting with a friend about choir practice, and Jimmy asking Jess to meet at the field. I could only listen a short while. I stuck a scissor into a plastic hole and pulled out yards and yards of thin brown filmy strips.

The Art of Persuasion

It was 3:30 a.m. and I was still awake in a guard dog mode. How could I know it and not know it. I mean the sexual tension seemed to be everywhere in the house. I searched for evidence and kept out of his office because . . . why? Because I had respect for his privacy? I hated Ray. I wanted to kill him. Every accusation, justified. I believed Tori when I knew she was lying and I believed Ray . . . whatever he said. A favorite book of his was the Art of Persuasion. And Ray could sell ice to an Eskimo.

I jumped out of bed, searched through the bookshelves, and found *The Art of Persuasion* with my nursing class picture, stuck in between the pages for a bookmark. I tore my smiling face into tiny pieces and dropped it into my robe pocket.

My scrambled brain attempted to figure this out. I needed to know. Where was I when he did these things to her? How did he even manage this when I seemed to keep track of everyone's whereabouts? Had he kept notes in the pages or margins of a book mapping out a plot, or was all this behavior etched only in his gray matter?

In the morning, I paced back and forth waiting for the phone to ring. And when it did, I couldn't think. Exhaustion and the inability to think set in simultaneously and I was blank for what seemed like a long time, but it was only seconds. My hands trembled. I blew out a smoke ring and ground my cigarette butt in the ashtray. On the fourth ring, I heard my own voice ask a question . . . *"Hello?"*

The treatment center had informed me upon admission that Ray was in group number five, which was considered the toughest of the tough group, with the hard-core addicts; and for that, I was enormously glad. Since Tori, Jimmy and I had to be intimately involved in Ray getting sober, reservations had already been made for a two-bedroom apartment across the street from the treatment center—the place we'd call home during Family Week.

"Hello there. This is the center calling from group number five for Emma. Ray is here with us, and first we need to check the sound. I want to make sure we can hear each other."

"Well, do you all hear me? I asked.

"Yes," answered strong men's voices.

"Good." Then I turned the receiver away from my ear and talked into the bottom part to make my announcement. "I'm only going to say this once. I want all of you to hear me. We will *not* be wasting our time. We will *not* be showing up. We are *not* participating. That's it! Amen."

"Wait, I don't understand," the group leader said.

"Really now . . . So, Ray hasn't told you what he did?"

"Ray?" the counselor asks. "Ray has shared with us about his drinking—it's called a *drunk-a-log*. There's more we need to hear?"

"You guys don't know the monster sitting with you. Ray honey, too chickenshit to tell the group you're a pervert? Ask him about his daughter! Ask him about his sex life with her—then you'll know who the lying son-of-a-bitch is . . ."

The counselor interrupted and overrode my voice, "Okay, this phone call is finished for now." The speakerphone squealed and a click on the line canceled out the echoes. "I will be contacting you. Thank you for your time."

The phone went dead. I slumped into the rocking chair and rocked back and forth for hours.

The next day, my whole body felt hollow after the center called back.

"I've talked to Ray. I know what he did to your daughter. We must talk in person."

"I've already told you, we are not coming."

He cleared his throat, and before he could add anything, I continued, "He can go to hell."

"I know you feel that way, but someone needs to help your family."

"Help? Someone was supposed to help us years ago and didn't. It's a little late I'd say!"

"That's what we do here, honest. We put families back together. I'm begging—let us help you. Do it for your daughter," he pleaded. "Please come."

How can getting us back together help? Is he crazy? His words bounced off the walls, slapping me in the face. Ray was so sick and the kids . . . Oh my god, I needed help. I hadn't dared tell anyone what had happened. I reached for a Kleenex and cleared my throat.

"Okay . . . Monday morning . . . we'll be there."

When I hung up, I didn't know what to do with myself. Jimmy was at a friend's house for an over-night. I called my sponsor in Al-Anon, but she wasn't home. Standing in front of the refrigerator, I chewed on a piece of cold pepperoni pizza. I brushed my teeth, stuck my tongue out at my reflection in the bathroom mirror, twisted my hair into a knot, and jammed an ivory comb into my scalp.

I ended up at an Al-Anon meeting, but didn't remember driving there through the heavy wet snow. Seven anonymous people sat in a dimly lit room. I held a tissue in my hand, stared at the candle in the middle of the table, and listened to the readings. I was depleted, empty and starving for something. This was where I got filled up with hope, and it usually worked for me, but not tonight. I tried to relate with their experiences but only shared that we would be participating in a family week. No judgments were made at meetings; no one told someone else what to do. People shared their own experiences, strength and hope, but no one talked about dads molesting their daughters. I felt hopeless tonight. Here we sat with ourselves, sullen-faced and full of pain. The aroma of coffee and peels of laughter that filtered through the adjacent doors of AA pissed me off. *Weren't they the cause of our problems?* I was angry they were laughing. I wanted them to hurt like I did.

"I can't seem to think straight," I said. "Everything takes more energy than I have."

After the meeting, the only man in our group said, "You're exhausted—sleep deprived. Get some rest."

I drove up Main Street. The lights on the theatre marquee blinked under a blanket of snow. I crept slowly past my childhood home, glancing up to see if the lights were on in my old bedroom. I had a lively imagination as a kid and pictured myself in a big city, but never ever did I imagine that I'd live up this same street in the two-story house on the corner, married with children. I never pictured pain in my life. *I wanted to live happily ever after, like Cinderella.*

I passed two blocks of darkened houses, and pulled into my driveway. Once in the house, I dropped my clothes on top of yesterday's. Tomorrow Tori would be home from college and join Jimmy and me at the treatment center for Family Week. I didn't brush my teeth. I didn't wash my face. I immediately dropped into bed.

Family Week

The trip in my little Chevy took four hours. I filled up halfway there, checked the oil and stopped for burgers. I stayed focused on the yellow line so my mind wouldn't wander and said *Hail Marys*—a whole rosaries worth on my fingers. Jimmy listened to his music.

I promised Tori I'd stick by her side through everything, and she agreed to meet us there. We walked in together. I held Tori's trembling hand when we stood in line in the lobby. We left our suitcases in the freezing car without noticing it was way below zero.

An old Seth Thomas school clock that hung on the wall caught my attention and briefly gave me a second's break, while the old globe light over the counter reminded me of grade school. I had never been to one of these places before.

Jimmy stood beside me fiddling with his broken shoelace. When he took off his parka, I noticed his misbuttoned shirt and nudged him. He nudged me back and scowled. He kicked my shoe but I let it go, since he hated me for dragging him here. In a loud whisper he said, "Mom, it's your fault. It's us against dad—three against one."

Tori pinched him and whispered something that made him shrug his shoulders fiercely.

A high, sickly-sweet voice greeted us with a smile. "Welcome. Here are the keys to your apartment. If we can be of assistance to you in any way, please let us know."

The entrance to our apartment was on the side of a stucco fourplex. We walked single file along a narrow, shoveled sidewalk with the snow piled high. We bumped the sides of the walls with our suitcases as we descended a steep stairwell to the basement. I unlocked the door and switched on the light. It was plain and clean, with two single beds and a fold-out couch. While I opened the window to vent a slightly musty odor in the kitchen, Jimmy snooped in drawers, looked behind pictures and picked up the rug. Tori unscrewed the bottom of the telephone.

"What the hell are you kids doing?"

"We want to see if it's bugged," they said.

I laughed first and then they howled. Jimmy shoved his sister and then he did it to me. We pushed each other around gently, still standing in our winter gear and dripping on their clean floor, but didn't care. None of us wanted to be there. I looked at my kids and knew I was their only hope now, and holding back this eerie release of emotions, I extended my arms, squeezing my kids as hard as I could, until they wiggled free.

"Will you please get along while I'm gone to this meeting?" They threw their jackets on the floor. "Tori, help Jimmy do his homework."

I blew them a kiss, pulled the door closed behind me, yelled, "Lock it!" and bounded up the stairs.

Orientation

People gathered in the large main hall. Everyone looked rather lost, so instead of melding into that group, I looked for the nearest fire exit, and sat with my back against the wall with a full view of pale yellow walls, wooden chairs in the center, and benches under scenic badland photos. Two scrolls, the Twelve Steps and the Twelve Traditions hung in simple, wide, black frames between two large windows. The reputation of this facility was one of the best in the Midwest. People flew in from California, Arizona and Idaho for treatment. Tonight, it was standing room only for adult family members.

A short man wearing a herringbone jacket greeted us in a voice that grated on me. He was what I called a *marshmallow man*: fluffy and soft. He was fat, but he wore a stiff suit and a starched shirt with a gold tie clip and cuff links. He patronized us with his pathetic expression. I didn't come here for his pity, and I sure in the hell didn't care where the vending machines were located. *Get me answers and get me out of here.* I shifted my weight from one leg to the other, sighed rudely and took in the serious faces around the room.

When the speaker addressed us, asking *"Why are you here?"* I leaned forward and bellowed from the back of the room, "I'm here because it's illegal to kill him. I've come to kick some ass!"

For a split second, it was dead silent; and then one person clapped, and then another, until everyone did—and some even whistled. People stood. One screamed, "I'm damn mad, too." Stomping feet made the floor rumble. The counselors began to whisper to one another, the lights came up, and the session ended with a huge circle and the recitation of the Serenity Prayer.

Exhausted, I headed across the street. I was no longer willing to be a victim.

Treatment

Over the next seven days, we endured hour-long grueling sessions. Life exposed to the bone was routine. Moreover, there was no physical contact allowed between anyone outside of these sessions. Conversations were public. Every night we returned to our apartment, went directly to bed, and in the early morning started all over again.

We witnessed the work of each member in the group and their families. In the center of the room, the addict sat on a hot seat. We were the last ones.

When Tori finally had the opportunity to confront her dad, there were lies, threats and tears. The Chaplain, like a gentle bulldozer, whisked Tori away for her protection. Tori made a choice to go—herself—to the local Sheriff's office with an escort the next day. The Sheriff accompanied Tori back to the treatment center with a warrant after she had made her official complaint of her molestation.

The Sheriff arrested Ray, handcuffed him, pushed his head down, and opened the back-seat car door.

I watched from behind a curtained window and heard him whine, *"But, I loved her . . ."*

His rounded shoulders made him look smaller, older and unthreatening until you saw the anger in his eyes. The arrest condition was that Ray had to complete his thirty-day treatment program for alcoholism, and twenty-four hours after discharge, report to jail for his criminal offenses.

After the arrest, Ray and I still had to participate in couple's counseling. Ray sat in an armchair with a clipboard and pen, finishing his homework assignment from our counselor. It took physical effort for me to sit still. The slight breeze from the hall brushed my flushed face, and my mind was heavy, like sludge. The arms attached to my heavy body rested at my side and I held my closed notebook in my lap. My homework was incomplete. I could not, for the life of me, come up with three reasons why I should stay with Ray.

"This is it," I said with clarity. I tore out my blank piece of paper, placed it on the seat of my chair and added, *"I'm finished."*

The door squeaked as I pushed it open, and when the counselor called my name, I kept walking and slipped my diamond off my finger and into my pocket.

On our final day, I checked under the beds and picked up literature on Alateen. Jimmy's glove was behind the television. Last night he threw it. *"How could you have Dad arrested?"* he screamed at Tori. *"Even the dog hates you!"* He nearly kicked a hole through the wall in the apartment.

I scrubbed off his boot print and straightened the crooked picture. Tori, exhausted and relieved, threw her clothes into a laundry bag.

"What about your dirty clothes?" I said.

"I'll do them at school. I just want to get out of here." Tori said.

I closed my suitcase, dumped the cold cigarette butts in the garbage and tossed the smelly, spotted bananas. I was ready to go.

The knock on the door was my counselor. "You're way too angry to leave here," he said staring at me. Tori jeered, her jaw locked so tight tears formed in her eyes.

I stared back noticing we were all the same height. "So what?" I said. I leaned against the door jamb. He put his hand on both of my shoulders and spoke softly to me.

"Your health insurance covers another week. What do you say, Emma?"

"I think I'm more screwed up than Ray?"

Tori wiped her face with her sleeve.

"I know it's not fair," he continued. "Please, look at me. Your kids want you to get better."

I bit my lip. "Okay; I'll stay. But only if you can help me through the rage."

"We can help you help yourself," he said, and left.

I unpacked my bag while Tori put Jimmy on a plane home to stay with his aunt and uncle. I sat there in this lifeless apartment, opened my notebook and wrote out the Serenity Prayer. I boiled water and opened a package of hot chocolate that I had stashed in my purse, smoked a few cigarettes and shut off the lights.

Once my mother said there was always someone worse off than you were, but this time it was not true. No other cases of molestation were reported. Pity crept in. I knew everyone wondered how this happened . . . wondered how I played a part in it. The suspicions sickened me because I was her mother, for God's sake. Shame and sorrow tossed me into a hatred that I didn't know was possible. I hated Ray and the heinous crime he violated against Tori. I had to get away—like I should have twenty years ago.

Professionally facilitated sessions addressed my anger hourly, and I sat knee-to-knee with Ray and screamed at him, releasing the feelings of his betrayal. I was broken down, empty, raw. Then there was a point where, with each hour that passed, I hung onto every word; and the counselors respectfully scooped me up, gave my strength back, and supported me. It was hard and I attended Twelve-Step meetings, wrote for hours in a journal, shared and listened to stories about lives, ate in the cafeteria with families, and prayed fervently, never leaving the facility until my seven days were over.

Cleaning House

When I returned home, a monster took up residence in my head. I slept poorly, drank too much coffee and smoked too many cigarettes. One day I drove down the street and saw two little girls at a card table. The bright tablecloth was too big and hung to the ground. They had a big pitcher in front of them next to their hand printed *'Lemonade For Sale'* sign. Several fresh lemons were stacked in a chipped, crystal bowl beside a tin can with a plastic lid for their money.

How sweet, I thought and parked on the other side of the street and watched. Then a bald man in a new, red Oldsmobile quickly pulled over. He bought a glass, sipped it slowly, smiled and laughed with them. When he left, a man in a station wagon did the same thing. He got out, chatted and sipped lemonade with them. *Was it they were thirsty or was it they got erections?!* When I tried to shake the thought, I started crying and couldn't stop.

~~~~

I called the FBI and they came to my house. They were interested in getting sexual perpetrators who crossed state lines. The Special Investigations Officer filled his car with cameras, guns, pornography magazines, notes on bits of paper, matchbooks, hotel receipts, all belonging to Ray. After their investigation, they returned everything, shy of getting Ray on any charges, because I had regretfully destroyed every picture of Ray with Tori that I had found in his office.

It was easy getting down in the dumps and I began to feel complacent and ready to give up, until I called my old college roommate, Zoe, who had been my matron of honor when I married Ray. We hadn't talked for years, but she had known Ray and I needed her. She listened carefully, and when I finished talking and my voice faded to a whisper, Zoe repeated back all the horrible things I had said that Ray had done to Tori; and when I heard the abuse in her voice, I became very upset . . . but, she had to repeat all that crap back to me.

"That's better, Emma . . . Stay angry. Anger is your friend!" she said—and I got it.

When Ray returned to town, he went directly to the jail, was fingerprinted, photographed in an orange jumpsuit, interviewed and given a period around the end of the month for sentencing. I first saw him when he was coming out of a Twelve-Step meeting on Broadway. The news of his arrest made the third page of the Herald; and even though it was an unlisted juvenile, everyone knew her name. People began to walk down different aisles at the store and pretend not to see me. I toughened up so I wouldn't crumble; and just in case someone actually was nice to me, I couldn't afford to fall apart.

Now I *needed* to be divorced quickly—before Ray went to prison. I pushed hard to make it happen because this stigma and shame was too difficult. My deceased father was not affected, but my mother was saddened when I came around. She felt sorry for me, and I hated this pity.

Ray quickly hid assets, dumped evidence of being crooked and shredded paperwork in his back office. He quickly sold off gold and silver, stashing the money into accounts that I was unable to locate. My lawyer did not believe me. I took things into my own hands and pretended Ray sent me in to pick up a package at the post office. I breathed a sigh of relief when I was able to intercept a sizable check behind his back. I hurried to my car, and as I was pulling out of the post office, Ray parked to go inside. I drove the back roads to the credit union, deposited the check, transferred funds into another account, and without suspicion, paid off both cars and a loan. He was furious when he discovered what I had done.

The Divorce

On the morning of my divorce hearing, I bought a classy, red dress with big, black buttons from the sale rack. It fit me perfectly and looked great with my black-patent heels. I wanted to stand tall and look confident, like I knew how to do this. I made the sign of the cross and smiled at my reflection in the elevator. Not bad, I thought. What bothered me the most was that my lawyer (what an ass) warned me again *not* to mention incest as a reason for this divorce, but to say *irreconcilable differences* and leave it at that. He said incest belonged in the court system dealing with Tori. I lost my opportunity to make a public statement, even if it was only in divorce court.

I had to have the divorce before Ray's sentencing. It was easier for me to have an *ex* go to prison than a husband. I needed the split, even though the property was still undecided. I noticed the lights on at the shop late at night and merchandise gone. I suspected "hidden" versus "sold."

I changed the locks on the house and moved Ray's personal belongings to the side yard.

Blessed are we who have people in Al-Anon for their support, a sponsor . . . a true friend, the type treasured forever. She greeted me with open arms, an open heart, great coffee and a never-ending supply of chocolate kisses in a bowl on her table.

I was a single, at last. Tori was happy, but confused and still felt sorry for her dad.

The Sentencing

The District Attorney's office informed me at work via phone, at 4:30 p.m. on a Friday, that the Judge added Ray's case to the docket for 4:45 p.m. that day—squeezed in right prior to the customary, month-long, summer vacation for the courts.

How could he do that? Tori wasn't even available to stand up for herself. She was at music camp in Canada. This was not fair.

I took off my cap and flew out the back door of the clinic. It was twenty blocks to Main Street and another six blocks to Broadway. I made it without getting a ticket and sat myself down in an empty courtroom. I stood when the judge in his black robe entered the room. A somber-faced court reporter was off to the right, and the District Attorney to my left, who represented Tori, placed a skimpy folder on the table in front of him.

This was unfair. Tori was supposed to be here and face her father in a court of law. It was part of the plan for her healing, but she was in Canada at music camp. If I hired a private plane, she couldn't even arrive in time. I tried to make eye contact with the Judge, but he didn't look at me.

Ray wore a new shirt. His eyes shifted around the air-conditioned room, and I was right in his line of vision in my nurse's uniform. My hands were clammy and I folded them together to keep from shaking. My white, polished shoes were getting tighter; my shoelaces choking me. I paid no attention, looked straight ahead and watched every move.

It was at 4:45 p.m. that Ray's lawyer leaned over and whispered to him and he chortled. After the case number was read, Ray pled guilty to three counts of Gross Sexual Behavior with his daughter, and immediately, the Judge charged Ray with incest and gave him a two-year sentence in the State Penitentiary. They seemed to take the whole situation lightly, giving Ray sixty days to put his business in order—and he was allowed to drive himself to prison and store his car until his release.

The Judge adjourned court, banged his gavel and exited the

room at exactly 5:00 p.m. Ray's lawyer closed his briefcase. The District Attorney wished everybody a nice summer vacation and slipped out the back way.

I was livid! *Who said three counts?* I slid to the edge of my seat in this surreal courtroom. *That was pure bullshit. And who came up with that absurd number?* From age nine to nineteen equals ten years . . . multiplied by 365 days! That was more like it. Ray took advantage of Tori every one of those days in some way. I stared at the wall. *How did this happen?*

The Altercation

It was early in the afternoon on the day Ray left for prison. His Town Car sat in the back of an electronics shop on Main Street. Curious, I parked out of sight, walked over and looked through the open car windows. On the front seat was a large manila envelope with an unknown bank address. It was the proof I needed for my lawyer. And resting between the seats was a small handgun, which was illegal for him to have in his possession. I grabbed both just as Ray came out the back door.

"Stop!" he yelled and charged after me.

I palmed the hand pistol and began to run, but I couldn't get any momentum in my sandals. He grabbed me hard and spun me around. With that jolt, we were face-to-face in an adrenalin standoff. Ray twisted my arm in snakebite, back and forth, burning my skin.

"Give me my gun . . . It's loaded!" he yelled.

"No! You can't have it."

"Give it to me, goddammit!"

"No!" I screamed, "HELP!" The entire parking lot was empty. No one was on the street—like a deserted city block on a movie set. I yelled repeatedly and fought back.

He let go of his grip and sprung forward. Ray got the package from me and flung it in the direction of his parked car. He dug his hard nails into the tops of my hands, breaking my skin. He was enraged and strong, ground his heels on the tops of my feet, and pulled my hair. Grunting and panting, he pulled me into him. Ray's sweat dripped on my mouth and I spat it back. Then he jerked my shoulder around and put my arm in a chickenwing, so my fingers touched the back of my head. With his face pressed hard against my cheek, he said, "*I never loved you, you stupid bitch!*" He forcefully grabbed the small pistol away. Then he swooped up the package, ran into the shop and pulled the steel door closed.

I didn't know how long I had sat in my car as the welts rose on my arms and feet. But tonight he would be sleeping behind bars and we would be safe.

The Answer to My Prayers

I was employed full time at the clinic attached to the hospital. I didn't know who knew what had happened. No one mentioned anything or asked questions.

Dr. Samuelson called me into his office on Friday and closed the door. "I'm leaving," he said. "I have been offered a position in the clinic of my hometown. My parents live there and I am thrilled to pieces." He held back giggles telling me.

I was happy for him, without knowing the devastating consequences.

All weekend I prayed and made a nine-hour Novena to St. Jude, the Patron Saint of Hopeless Cases, mostly because it kept my mind busy. I was sad to lose my doctor and I needed some personal direction in my life. I checked the clock every hour, dropped down on my knees, got myself to another Al-Anon meeting, and surrounded myself with friends.

Monday morning I was called into the office of the Clinic Manager, but it wasn't the usual person. It was a newly hired troubleshooter, working out a financial fitness plan at the request of the doctors, and I seemed to fit into the scheme of things. It was a depressed economy and I was a full-time RN with benefits and a pension. They cut my position. Since my doctor was moving, they had no use for me, and the troubleshooter's plan was to hire a part-time LVN with a considerable savings to the clinic. They didn't tell me that, but it wasn't hard to figure. They laid me off. The going away coffee and cake party in the employees' lounge was for both of us, since Dr. Samuelson was also leaving.

I felt much older than forty standing in line at the unemployment office. I completed paperwork and made daily phone calls but was never called for an interview. As the time went on, I stood in the food line with people I had once helped and got my government cheese. I collected my small stipend and continually attempted to find work. Since I was no longer able to make the mortgage payments now, I lost the house. I opened the closets and drawers and started sorting and throwing for a yard sale and auction.

I started life over. But I needed a plan.

One Day at a Time

I couldn't sleep in the bed I shared with Ray, where he had raped Tori. I spent long, restless nights on a brown, corduroy couch in the bedroom. It was after midnight when I threw off the covers, took a sip of water, and lit up a cigarette.

Occasionally, a car drove by—their lights arched across the ceiling. I rolled, tossed and prayed. I begged God for help. I squeezed my tangled rosary beads in my fingers so tight they made gouges. Right then, while I prayed, my heart flipped in my chest. I was scared, placed both hands over my left breast, and held my breath. I was wide-eyed awake. I lie perfectly still and listened. It was the quietness. It was quieter than I'd ever heard. It was the rest between my heartbeats. My shoulders dropped down and relaxed. My warm breath escaped in small musical notes. I had no words to describe how my worries vanished or what it was like being wrapped in something invisible like a cocoon.

In the morning, when I woke from my first restful sleep, I *knew* I had the presence of God as close to me as my breath. Those few moments were the early beginnings of my recovery.

∞

Try to Erase the Past

My wedding gown hung in a sealed bag at the top of the stairs in a cedar closet. I was going to make sure Tori never wore this dress. Sitting down on the top step, I rubbed the satin against my cheek. I laughed for a second, remembering the sound of my dress sleeve splitting as I hugged my aunt. I put my fingers into the same hole, stood on the hem with my bare feet and pulled hard, tearing through the designer satin. I finished it off with a scissors, cut the dress into long strips, tied them into knots and bows and piled them on the worn carpet of the landing. My fingers cramped, I cried and snot dripped and soaked the material, but I couldn't stop making piles. I put the empty, padded hanger back in the closet and splashed cold water on my face.

The kids came out of their bedrooms and helped, stacking the bundles in my arms without saying a word. Their faces twisted into an expression that might have said I was a little off; but I smiled, stood straight up, marched out into the back yard, and dumped the mass of cloth, pearl beads and all, into the garbage barrel, determined to erase my past.

I came up with another idea one afternoon at my sponsor's house. We finished our fourth cup of coffee and polished off a half a bowl of chocolate candy kisses between talking about recovery. But I was getting restless and daring. "Will you go to the little corner grocery store with me?"

"What do you need? I might already have it," she said.

"No . . . I can't explain it. You'll see what I mean . . . it's for Tori and Jimmy and me."

We walked down the street. I greeted the woman behind the penny candy counter, worked my way passed the canned goods to the back of the store, and stood in line. This little store, noted for its fine meats always had customers. When it was my turn at the meat counter, I pointed to the biggest hot dogs.

"Four pounds of those plumped wieners," I demanded, ". . . the dogs connected like a rope."

He held one up. "Like this far down . . . or here?" he asked.

"Separate them, and then chop each single dog in half, please."

He looked puzzled.

I kept a steady level gaze at the butcher in the bloodstained apron. I couldn't tell if he was a nice man or someone also living a lie. My friend moved closer to me. We watched the whiny, high-pitched rotary blade buzz off the chunks of wieners shooting them onto the butcher block. I wanted to castrate everything in the place, but I couldn't afford it. When the butcher finished, I thanked him and paid, then I walked over to the garbage barrel in silence and dropped the waxed paper bundle in the can. My friend looped her arm through mine. We laughed all the way home, and through the power of observation and imagination, a little piece of me was healed.

While Jimmy dug around and sorted things of his to sell, he found a Ziploc bag filled with white powder. I called the police and told them we were coming to the station, which was only a few blocks away. But just in case of a violation, or if someone crashed into me, I wanted them to know . . . *we found it*! We sat down with the police officer who had met us at the door and he said it was a bag of methamphetamine. The undercover cops weren't surprised. They had been watching Ray for months in an attempt to get him on drug sales, but on the day of the scheduled bust, the police said Ray got wind of something and refused to sell to their agent. The investigation failed.

My anger continued to fuel my energy and catapulted me

into action. I did something every day for myself between crying, and recited the Serenity Prayer like a mantra under my breath and with every footstep: "*God grant me the serenity to accept the things I cannot change, the Courage to change the things I can **and** the wisdom to know the difference.*"

It was right before Ray's first parole hearing that he sent Tori flowers and a stuffed animal with hearts on it.

"Thanks Mom," Tori said when she called from her dorm.

I immediately figured out her dad was up to something from behind the bars.

"Tori, I didn't send it!"

She cried like a small child and the vase crashed to the floor.

The warden listened and explained that volunteers will often buy gifts for the inmates to give on the outside, but this clearly broke the issued restraining order placed on Ray. *Parole denied!*

When I told the story to my friends while having coffee at Pappy's, Juno, a huge man who said he owed his recovery to helping people, volunteered to have Ray *whacked* in prison, or gang raped, if it was my pleasure. The thought was pleasant for a few minutes, but I couldn't give my approval.

I learned that from the minute Tori was born, or even perhaps before that, Ray established a systematic method for sexual grooming. His hugs and kisses were sensual and suggestive. He kept each of us separated and controlled our interactions. Ray claimed no remorse or guilt for the heinous behaviors against Tori. Ray used us, lied to us, manipulated and seduced us. He betrayed our trust and called it love.

Ray served eighteen months of a two-year sentence because in the prison system, one year equals nine months. The restraining order against him for Tori was for five years.

Today, Ray, a sexual predator *before* Megan's Law, lives free.

Epilogue

After Ray was put away, Tori entered into treatment for Alcoholism, which helped right our relationship. Today she has twenty-five years clean and sober. I combined my Al-Anon meetings with continued Mass attendance and began to learn how to take care of myself.

My friend Zoe invited me to California to see if I would like to move there, and my life was suddenly happening. I arrived on the Monterey Peninsula on Easter Monday, attended an Al-Anon meeting that evening, and collected phone numbers from recovering people who asked me to call them anytime.

The next day I job hunted, had an interview, one in person and the other over the telephone from a long-term care facility that needed a Director of Nursing. I was starting in two weeks. I rented a new condominium in the village by the beach, only minutes from work.

I had my plan: sell everything and start over. I would change everything about myself, except the way I tore my checks out of my checkbook.

The auctioneer I had come to know had a sister in California, who wanted him to visit, so we helped each other out. He drove my car loaded up with the essentials like my coffee pot, toaster, breakfast dishes and my wooden crucifix, to San Jose. He stood inside Gate C-12, waiting when I landed. He gave me a hug, introduced me to his sister, and we exchanged my keys for his plane fare. It was a smooth transition.

In the Midwest, Jimmy had attended a school located right across the street from St. Joseph's Church and six blocks from our house. Here in California, Jimmy enrolled in a middle school located across from another St. Joseph's church and six blocks from our condo.

Jimmy was disappointed when he had to leave his friends, but after the first week living here, he made new ones. He met friends from divorced parents and not much was made over not having a dad. Every day I told Jimmy he was special. Each night I put my arms around him while he stood rigid, arms at his side with his face turned away. A breakthrough happened a couple of years later. I kissed Jimmy on his cheek and he unexpectedly wrapped his arms around *me.* It was worth my effort and the long wait to have my heart melt once again.

Concerned with a fear of falling into further dysfunction, Tori, Jimmy and I agreed to deal with our emotions. We made a pact, swearing no matter how hard life became, suicide would never be an option. During that time of change and adjusting, we saw professionals, attended Twelve-Step programs and believed in God. Our mirrors no longer reflected victims. We became a strong family. We for damn sure weren't going to tell anyone we had been in hell and we weren't going back.

Jimmy got jobs, starting at age fourteen, repairing bicycles; then he did dishes at the Bandstand and talked on the telephone in a marketing firm. He met people and established good work ethics at a young age. He bought his first car for a dollar and sold it for five hundred dollars. By age seventeen, he had left home and went on to make more stories that are his to tell, not mine. Today he runs a successful business, is married with two sons and a daughter, and I am proud of him.

Ray's monthly salary went into a prison savings account, and he worked in the kitchen with other sexual perpetrators, separated from the general population. He wrote Jimmy a letter that was nearly impossible to read because the tiny words were spread over every inch of the paper. Once Jimmy answered him, he never received another. I fought for child support through the California District Attorney's office, and eventually a small check came for Jimmy, and Ray settled his debt.

Tori stayed in college, flew out West for breaks and vacations, and helped Jimmy and me move to a new apartment. She set up the kitchen just the way she knew we'd like it. She said it made her feel special, like she was maintaining her family ties. She spent the first night alone, and the next morning, welcomed Jimmy and I with a tour of the cupboards.

Tori had an incredible senior recital and graduation that I attended with my mother and my aunt. Tori's fiery passion for music helps kids develop their talents. She is a wholesome, spiritual woman, a teacher, conductor and well-known in her community. She is happily married to a fine man and has two teenaged sons.

I always wanted her to know how much I loved her and how sorry I was that I was unable to protect her. I guess Tori put up with about as much as she could before she sat me down and let me have it!

"Mom, when we're together, you act like it happened yesterday!"

"What?"

"Think about it Mom . . ."

"Oh my god . . . I didn't . . . I mean, I'm sorry."

"Don't apologize . . . just stop it. It's been twenty-five years now."

Afterword

What occurred *under my roof* wouldn't leave me. It remained a restless, stirring in my gut. I could not erase it or stand on the street corners and bellow it out, so I re-lived my life in the narrative. It was with nonjudgmental support from a writing group led by Ellen Bass that I revealed my nearly unbearable truth.

Now, I am no longer afraid. I have no secrets and the cycle of violence has ended.

My wish is that other *Mothers of Survivors* find consolation, peace, love and joy. It is possible. I know that because now those gifts live, *Under My Roof.*

This is my story.

I wrote it for you.

I wrote it for me.

~ 🌸 ~

Resources

Valuable Information for Prevention, Support and Education:

MASA   Mothers Against Sexual Abuse
www.againstsexualabuse.org

MOSAC   Mothers of Sexually Abused Children
www.mosac.net

RAINN   Rape Abuse Incest National Network
www.rainn.org

SHC   Survivors Healing Center
www.survivorshealingcenter.org

Kidpower ™
Kidpower Teenpower Fullpower International
    – Child Abuse and Bullying Prevention
    – Stranger Awareness and Personal Safety
    www.kidpower.org

Documentaries and movies:
    Boyhood Shadows - PBS
    Jane, the movie [1]

Note: Author and publisher have made every effort to provide accurate internet addresses at the time of publication, but neither the author nor the publisher assume any responsibility for errors or changes after the date of publication nor assume any responsibility for content of third-party websites.

---

1   At the time of publication of this book, *Jane, the movie* is in production. visit www.jane-themovie.com

Reader Conversation Guide to Facilitate
Book Club Discussions

Thank you for making *Under My Roof, A Mother's Story of the Heinous Crime of Incest* part of your book club readings. When we stop the silence, sexual abuse may end. These suggested questions are meant to facilitate an open discussion, raise awareness and further the healing process.

❖ This story took place in the 1960s, '70s and '80s. How have things changed since then?

❖ How would you have helped Emma?

❖ What part of this book was the most meaningful to you?

❖ Knowing what you know now, what is the first thing you would have done?

❖ What can we learn from this story? Have you had any experience in this area?

❖ Did this author succeed in raising your awareness about survivors and mothers?

❖ What were some of the "red flags" in the relationship?

❖ Do you watch television programs like *Frontline's*, "Rape in the Fields"?

Blessings,
Emalou King

~ *Notes* ~

~ ✥ ~

~ *Notes* ~

~ ❦ ~

~ Notes ~

~ Notes ~

~ 🙶 ~

~ Notes ~

~ ⚜ ~

About the Author

Emalou King, RN, BSN, Phn is a Registered Nurse with a Bachelors Degree and a Certificate in Public Health. She has worked in hospitals, clinics, nursing homes and drug treatment programs. The last sixteen years of King's nursing career involved drug-addicted mothers, their babies and preemies from Packard Children's Hospital at Stanford, as well as pregnant and parenting teens from the age of twelve and up.

Under My Roof ~ A Mother's Story of the Heinous Crime of Incest is a personal experience of deceit. When King started over out West, she kept her family secrets from friends, clients and colleagues because of shame and embarrassment. She hopes to convince you to believe that when a mother knows something is amiss, there is something amiss. When a mother thinks something is wrong . . . something is wrong. King is a mother in pursuit of truth, justice, advocacy and education in the prevention of child sexual abuse.

King has been published in the *Canadian Journal of Nursing*, contributed to the Mosby's textbook *Pharmacological Aspects of Nursing,* won the NDSNA writing contest twice and is the author of two paperback children's books. She dabbles in poetry and is interested in screenplay/script writing.

Follow Emalou King's blog: **http://emalouking.blogspot.com**
Email Emalou: **emalouking@aol.com**